THE

Theology of New England.

AN

ATTEMPT TO EXHIBIT THE DOCTRINES NOW PREVALENT IN THE ORTHODOX CONGREGATIONAL CHURCHES OF NEW ENGLAND.

BY DAVID A. WALLACE,
Boston.

WITH AN INTRODUCTION

BY DANIEL DANA, D. D.

BOSTON:
CROCKER AND BREWSTER,
47, Washington Street.
1856.

ADVERTISEMENT.

In the following pages, the author has attempted to state the Theology prevalent in the Congregational Churches of New England usually styled "orthodox." His aim has been to aid inquirers, whether in New England or out of it, who have not access to the original sources of information, in coming to a knowledge of the facts. While he has been careful to ascertain the truth, and state it clearly, he cannot flatter himself, that he has perfectly succeeded. Any mistakes, however, into which he has fallen, when pointed out, he will be most happy to correct.

INTRODUCTION.

It is generally admitted as a fact, that the Scriptures of God utter their great and saving truths in much simplicity and plainness. Miracles, it is confessed, are not excluded; but these miracles are propounded, not so much to our reason, as to an unquestioning and child-like faith. Far from obscuring the doctrines at large, they set them in their purest light, and reveal them in their heavenly beauty, and glory, and harmony.

Yet, paradoxical as it may seem, their very simplicity has proved a fruitful occasion of their being misunderstood and misrepresented. Speculative men, men of acute minds, and reasoning talents, coming to the Bible, and finding there nothing which a well-instructed child cannot understand nearly as well as themselves, are dissatisfied and disgusted. Hence *philosophy* is summoned to supply the defects, and adorn the artlessness, of scripture. But the attempt is fatal. By these devices, men's minds are unhinged, reason takes the place of faith, and endless doubts and misgivings are substituted for positive and satisfying certainty. Breaking loose from the eternal truths of God, men are seduced into a labyrinth of interminable and destructive error.

When we read the Epistles of St. Paul, we find that he rebuked this arrogant species of philosophy, viewing it as eminently and irreconcilably hostile to the pure truths of the gospel. In one passage, he brands it with the epithet of *science falsely so called.* And most justly. For what a wretched thing is that science which understands every thing but the truth of God, and the way of human salvation. How mis-called is that philosophy which arrays itself against divine and everlasting truth. *Genuine* philosophy is modest and unassuming. It delights to open its eyes to the light of heaven. It finds its most honorable and delightful place at the feet of Jesus. While the proud and self-sufficient reasoner, feeling no need of divine instruction, turns away from heavenly light, and clinging to the feeble taper of his own reason, wanders in the path leading to eternal darkness and eternal death.

These remarks are strongly confirmed by a signal passage in the New Testament history. The great Apostle of the Gentiles spent some days at Athens, a city which was not only the boasted light of Greece, but the seat of a great portion of the science, art, literature, and refinement which then existed in the world. And what was the Apostle's success in this favored spot? Less, probably, than in any other which was visited with his preaching. For while in some regions, comparatively dark and uncultivated, he witnessed many trophies of divine grace, his success in Athens was so small, that a few scattered individuals comprise the whole catalogue of his converts.

In modern times, the experiment of the power of reason, when divorced from Revelation, has been conspicuously made in Germany. In that favored land, the birth-place of Luther and the Reformation, who would not have wished that pure religion might have lingered for many a century? But such wishes have been sadly disappointed. About a century since, there arose there certain philosophers who, closing their eyes to the light of Heaven, and trampling on the teachings of the Bible, determined to make a religion for themselves, and for the community. They were men not destitute of genius, or of learning, or of research. Still less were they wanting in self-confidence. But they were awfully destitute of that humility to which Heaven is used to confine its holy light and aid. Their project was attended with fatal success. Being followed by a long line of successors of their own spirit, they poured darkness on the public mind; *darkness which might be felt*, and which is actually felt at the present day. Under its baleful influence, men of knowledge and refinement have yielded themselves to religious absurdities which would disgrace the lowest state of society. Germany witnesses at this day, in her Universities, her Theological Seminaries, and in her pulpits, men conspicuous for infidelity. The consequence of this state of things is natural and inevitable. The whole land is deluged with error and infidelity, with vices and crimes. We are recently informed, indeed, of some appearance of a revulsion. It is announced that men of sound minds and sound theology are lifting a powerful voice against the errors and abomination of the time; and that they find listeners too. Still may it not require a century, or even more, to repair the ravages which have been made on the cause of truth, and the intellects of the community?

Hence arises a question of no common interest. What is the influence which German theology has exercised for years, and is now exercising, on the theology of our own country? Of the reality of this influence, and of its extent, there can be no doubt. The simple fact that our young preachers, either at the commencement of their course, or in their preparation for it, are so prone to resort to that country, speaks an intelligible language. On this subject, we need not adopt a strain of indiscriminate reproof. A variety of motives and of circumstances may operate in the case. The history, geography and chronology of the Scriptures; their criticism, literature and antiquities, all have their importance and use. In these departments, the German religionists have exhibited indefatigable activity, and amassed immense stores of knowledge. Of these accumulations, religious students may safely and wisely avail themselves. Yet if, in these pursuits, their minds should be insensibly drawn away from the great and distinguishing *doctrines* of scripture, or should receive perverse or indistinct impressions of them, the evil would be immense. The largest acquisitions of such knowledge would but ill compensate for the want or loss of the essential and saving truths of God's word.

The attribute of Scripture which preëminently stamps its value and importance, is its Inspiration. Here lies the basis of all the instruction; the hope and comfort which it imparts. To renounce this precious attribute, is to give up ourselves to endless doubt and blank despair. While to have our faith in it shaken, or impaired, is to want the first and most essential qualification of christian instructors. Surely no one will contend that our young men, destined to the ministry, and subjected to the influences we have described, are in no danger of contamination.

Another source of danger to our country is found in the introduction of German writings. These, within a few years, have been imported to our land in a profusion formerly unknown. For about a century past, Germany has been the grand corrupter of Europe and the world. By its novels and poetry, and false philosophy, by its rationalism, and pantheism, and atheism, (for pantheism is substantially atheism,) it has spread havock through the morals and religion of Europe. For a long period, however, this great and tremendous evil was much confined to the more speculative and literary circles. But in more recent time, the language being better understood, and translations being abundantly multiplied, the evil has had a far more extensive diffusion, and found its way to all classes of society. And it cannot be sufficiently deplored, that the case is substantially the same in the country in which we live. Formerly, these skeptical and infidel notions were chiefly broached in books designed for speculative readers. But more recently, they find a place in writings intended for all classes, not excepting the most ignorant and uncultivated. So that, as we are become a nation of readers, these last bid fair to become as thorough proficients in infidelity as their superiors. And it must be confessed that in this school, they are often willing and docile students. Few, probably, are aware of that awful deterioration of religious views, feelings and practice which has swept over New England within the last thirty or forty years, and which threatens to sweep away every thing worthy the name of religion. One thing is certain. *Unbelief is the order of the day; the fatal malady of the age.* That religion which our pilgrim fathers brought with them, which they cherished as their dearest possession, and which they grasped to their hearts in life and in death, is, by thousands of their descendants, ignored, or denied, or treated with neglect and contempt.

It cannot be denied that the great and distinguishing doctrines of the gospel are, by thousands of our christian community, disbelieved and contradicted; perhaps despised and ridiculed. Other thousands there are, who, at some period of their lives, have solemnly declared their belief in them. Their hearts, however, were never truly reconciled to them. And finding that they are much opposed, especially in the fashionable world, and that much can be plausibly said and reasoned against their truth, they rejoice to employ these things as pretexts for discarding them altogether, and thus escaping their humbling and painful influence.

A third class value themselves on holding their judgment in suspense between these doctrines and their opposites. This, they contend, is dictated by candor and impartiality. They hold that on these topics, the Bible itself is obscure and indecisive; not fitted to give satisfaction to inquiring minds. Yet what is this but virtually to allege that the Book of God has been given us in vain; that while possessing a Revelation from God, we need another revelation to explain it, and that that inspired volume, which was designed to guide us to truth and heaven, is wholly incompetent to its object, and has utterly failed in its effect.

We may not neglect a fourth class of the religious in our community. It is composed of those who firmly believe, and cordially love, the distinguishing doctrines of the gospel—doctrines at once lying at its foundation, and manifest on the surface. On these doctrines hang their immortal hopes, and from them they derive their best consolations. At the same time, they are surrounded by multitudes by whom these truths are ignored, or disregarded, or opposed, or treated with scorn. Yet they withhold from these truths their open and vigorous support. Here is an inconsistency which we cannot sufficiently lament. And surely it will not always last. These good men must ultimately come forward, and, bitterly lamenting their past defects, throw all their weight and influence on the side of God's despised truth. May Heaven grant that this "consummation" so "devoutly to be wished" may not come too late.

There is a class of religionists in our community yet unmentioned. They hold that Christians at large are generally agreed; at least that they maintain no discrepancies in views which may not be easily merged. Let mutual candor and conciliation be cherished, and all will be well. To *contend earnestly* for particular doctrines, is needless and useless, and tending only to evil. Let this disposition subside, and Christians will remain in harmony, and the church in peace.

This train of thought is extremely plausible. But it is not more plausible than dangerous. It is proper, then, to give it a careful scrutiny.

The great and absorbing question before the christian public is this: do the doctrines which have been fashionable, and which are rapidly increasing in prevalence and extent, agree with the oracles of truth? In other words, are they the same doctrines which the church has, in every age, found in the Bible?

It has been well remarked that *deceit lies in generals.* To come at the truth, then, we must descend to particulars.

The Bible declares, explicitly and uniformly declares the *entire and awful depravity of man;* a depravity, which, descending from the first progenitor of the race, has infected all his offspring. This is the doctrine which pervades the Scripture from beginning to end. The doctrine is strictly fundamental. It lies at the basis of the structure on which human salvation is built. It gives character, complexion and features to all the doctrines and provisions of the gospel. It directly follows, that as this doctrine is received or rejected, the gospel itself is received or rejected. It cannot then be denied, that on this very spot, error, essential error is chargeable on the modern theology. It repudiates a cardinal doctrine of the Bible. It denies and discards *original sin* in the sense in which it has been understood and maintained by the church of God in all ages. That there may be no mistake on this vital point, we quote from the writings of a professor in the most important theological seminary of New England; a gentleman well known as the chief Expounder and Advocate of the new system. In a note appended to his Convention Sermon, he writes as follows:

"Is it said, that a passive nature, existing antecedently to all free action, is itself, strictly, literally sinful? Then we must have a new language, and speak, in prose, of moral *patients* as well as moral agents, of men *besinned* as well as sinners, (for *ex vi termini* sinners as well as runners must be active;) we must have a new conscience which can decide on the moral character of dormant conditions, as well as of elective preferences; a new law, prescribing the very *make* of the soul, as well as the way in which this soul, when made, shall act, and a law which we transgress (for sin is 'a transgression of the law') in being before birth passively mis-shapen; we must also have a new Bible, delineating a judgment scene in which some will be condemned, not only on account of the deeds which they have done in the body, but also for having been born with an involuntary proclivity to sin, and others will be rewarded not only for their conscientious love to Christ, but also for a blind nature inducing that love; we must, in fine, have an entirely different class of moral sentiments, and have them disciplined by Inspiration in an entirely different manner from the present; for now the feelings of all true men revolt from the assertion, that a poor infant dying, if we may suppose it to die, before its first wrong preference, *merits* for its unavoidable nature, that eternal punishment, which is threatened, and justly, against the smallest real *sin*. Although it may seem paradoxical to affirm that 'a man may believe a proposition which he knows to be false,' it is yet charitable to say that whatever any man may suppose himself to believe, he has in fact an inward conviction, that 'all sin consists in sinning.'"

It is needful here to remark, though the remark is uttered with inexpressible pain, that the author of the foregoing paragraph has repeatedly declared his assent to the Westminster Assembly's Shorter Catechism, and as often solemnly engaged to conform his instructions to that Summary of doctrine; expressly discarding the doctrine of Pelagianism. It is needless to add, that if the essence of Pelagianism consists in the denial of the native depravity of man, that signal error is plainly couched in the paragraph cited.

It is not denied that the *term* depravity is admitted into the new theology. But, wonderful as it may seem, it is represented as a *sinless* depravity. But who sees not that this is an abuse of terms? But why should such an abuse be admitted, tending only to vitiate and confound language, and to darken a subject which demands the utmost plainness and perspicuity?

With the doctrine of native depravity, that of *Regeneration* holds a close alliance. Indeed they involve each other. Nor is it less evident that the views entertained of the one, will greatly modify our views of the other. This we should naturally anticipate; and this is found to be the literal fact. If man is but partially depraved, a partial regeneration is all which he needs. If only nominally depraved, a nominal regeneration is sufficient to meet his case. Accordingly, the advocates of the new doctrine, while they admit the term regeneration, eviscerate it of all its meaning and force. They do not admit that it involves either a *holy* change, or a change of *nature*. As to the former point; contending, as they do, that all holiness as well as sin, consists in action; and allowing, as they must, that all holy action in the creature is preceded by regeneration, they cannot surely find holiness in regeneration itself. Maintaining that Adam, as he came from his Creator's hand, was not holy till he began to act, must they not maintain, that those regenerated by the Spirit are not holy till they begin to act? As to the other point, they deny that human beings are, properly speaking, depraved in *nature*. Where then is the necessity, where even the possibility of their being regenerated? And what a strange and nondescript kind of regeneration must that be, which passes on creatures not in their nature depraved and sinful.

As to the theory that all sin and holiness consist in action, or exercise, though it assumes the proud name of philosophy, we submit that it is as contrary to sound philosophy as to common sense and the Bible. There are certain states or conditions of the mind which belong, not to the class of volitions, but of principles, propensities, dispositions, or affections. But they are not, therefore, divested of a decidedly moral character. It would be absurd to contend that *pride* is a volition. Yet pride, by universal consent, is the most odious of vices. Nor would it be easy to prove that *humility* is a volition. Yet in the judgment of God himself, humility is the loveliest of virtues.

The doctrine of Justification by faith has ever been viewed by the church, in its best days, as a doctrine of the clearest evidence, and the deepest interest. What the great Luther thought of its importance is well known. Our puritan fathers guarded it with a sleepless vigilance, and zealously resisted every attempt to corrupt its purity. It has not been altogether so with their descendants. Within a century or less, this doctrine has lost much of the attention and respect which it claims. Many divines of some reputation have treated it with great neglect. Others, it should seem, have scarcely found it in the Bible. While others have manifested a wish to expunge it from the list of christian doctrines. From the modern theology it has experienced much disregard and opposition. The treatment which it has recently received, would, had it appeared half a century since, have been regarded with astonishment, not to say with horror. That Christ our Savior, being man, so needed obedience for himself as to have no merit to impart to his believing people; that the imputation of his righteousness is an absurdity; and that men must look to their own holiness and obedience to bring them to heaven—

these are among the dreams which are now extensively propagated. Thus the proud and self-righteous are propped up in their own imaginary goodness; and thus the self-diffident and humble are plunged into a species of despondence, and even despair.

It is much to be wished, that those who deny, and perhaps denounce the imputation of Adam's sin to his posterity, and Christ's righteousness to his believing people, would carefully study the fifth chapter of Romans. Doubtless they would discover that these doctrines are stamped with the same divine authority; that both the one and the other are equally and truly doctrines of the Bible. "As by the offence of one, judgment came upon all men to condemnation; even so by the righteousness of one, the free gift came upon all men unto justification of life. For as by one man's disobedience many were made sinners, so by the obedience of one shall many be made righteous."

We have no satisfaction in multiplying these reproofs, though some of our remarks may appear unduly severe. But there is still a topic of some interest deserving a serious attention.

For many years past, the subject of man's *ability* and *inability* has been much discussed, both in the sacred desk and in other scenes of instruction. Arguments on each side, almost equally plausible, and almost equally valid, are arrayed in mutual opposition. Still the debate continues;

and still the minds of men remain either in anxious uncertainty, or in unreasonable confidence.

The truth is, that questions on this subject are much less likely to be decided by philosophic reasoning, than by common sense and the Bible.

Still there are truths in the case, the force of which most candid minds will admit. That all human beings are under immediate and everlasting obligations to repent of their sins, to obey the law and receive the gospel—that there is no obstacle in the way, but such as arises from their own obstinacy and wickedness—and that their perdition, if they finally perish, will be of their own procuring; these are unquestionable facts.

It is equally unquestionable that sinners lie wholly at the mercy of God; that he holds their salvation and perdition in his own sovereign hand; and that all their efforts to save themselves will be utterly abortive, without divine and omnipotent aid.

Between these two classes of propositions there may be seeming discrepancies. But they are only seeming. All truths are reconcilable with all other truths. What appears to our frail minds to be discordant, may be quite otherwise in the eye of an omniscient God. And we ourselves, in a future state, may see clear and satisfying light, where now we behold only impenetrable darkness.

The propensity of the present day seems to be to magnify human power. Thoughts are sported on this subject, obviously irreconcilable with Scripture and common sense. This is undoubtedly a serious evil. For though these views seemingly tend to excite men to action, their real tendency is to lull them into sloth and security. Let a man believe that his salvation is fully, and in every sense, in his own power, and he will delay the disagreeable task to a more convenient season. He will become proud, self-sufficient, and careless. It is worth a serious inquiry, whether that recklessness as to religion and the soul, and even that laxity in principles and morals which so lamentably prevail in our day, are not attributable to extravagant views of human power and sufficiency.

On the topic thus briefly discussed, there arise some reflections too important to be neglected or forgotten. The error in question respecting human ability was, in former times, inculcated by ministers of great seriousness and fidelity—men who, in their private speculations, cherished sound and scriptural views on many gospel subjects; and who, in their public instructions, uttered many things suited to alarm the fears, and awaken the consciences, of the impenitent. But the case is otherwise now. The modern theology is superficial and unimpressive. It contains little which tends either to awaken the consciences, or alarm the fears of the irreligious. Of course, the error in question is left unqualified and unchecked, to produce its disastrous effects on the minds of men, and lead them insensibly in the path to ruin.

Concerning many of the errors which we have noted, it may be thought, perhaps, that they arise less from substantial deviations, than from mere changes in terminology. But to this grave remark, we reply in brief, that *words are things.* A slight change of terms may communicate very false impressions. We have likewise a right to enter a solemn protest against a new, unauthorized and inaccurate use of language. It is not fit, that in this way, the instructions of the pulpit should become unintelligible, the minds of men filled with confusion, and the religious public kept in a state of unceasing agitation.

But perhaps the case demands an attention and statement still more serious. Can it be for a moment denied that, within a few years, words have so entirely changed their meaning, that the christian pulpit emits darkness rather than light? Can it be denied that the terms *Depravity*, *Conversion*, *Regeneration*, *Atonement*, *Justification*, etc., have lost their original sense, and assumed a meaning altogether new? Can it be denied, that in the principal Theological Seminary of New England, the religion taught is depravity without sin, regeneration without holiness, and justification without the righteousness of Christ? Can it be denied, that pious hearers often retire from the sanctuary, and from the instructions of a preacher whose leading views are entirely opposite to their own, yet honestly believing that they have heard the very gospel which they loved? Can it be denied, that *different classes* of hearers, *widely distant* in sentiment, have each come away in the confidence that the preacher was of their own opinion?

In these cases, charity would perhaps forbid us to suspect that the preacher has harbored a direct intention to deceive. Perhaps his aim has been to exhibit truths so modified and ornamented as that they shall neither displace the tasteful and philosophic, nor disgust the worldly, nor repel the open enemies of religion. But surely it cannot be sufficiently lamented, that the pious should be defrauded of the food on which they feast and live; the consciences of sinners left undisturbed, the unbelieving confirmed in their infidelity, and the hypocrite and self-deceived encouraged in their ruinous delusions.

Where are the Christians who have occupied this stage for twenty or thirty years, and have not witnessed a real *revolution* in religion—in its doctrinal views, its experience and its practice? The wide and perceptible distance once existing between the pious and the impenitent is almost annihilated. The irreligious are prone to imagine that they are half as good as Christians; the church, instead of communicating its stamp to the world, receives from the world its own stamp; and the really pious are too often lost in the crowd.

The decline and abandonment of the truth, so prevalent and undeniable, have unquestionably sunk our churches into a sadly depressed condition. That lukewarmness, formality and awful defections are found in thousands of professed Christians is generally admitted. The fact, too, appears to be generally lamented. It is one of the wonders of the time, that the close connection that exists between these two grand evils, seems to be rarely traced and acknowledged. Yet how can it be expected that evils will be removed until they are distinctly seen—seen in their causes and connection, as well as in their magnitude and aggravations? Should it please God, in his holy sovereignty, to visit our community with the influences of his Spirit, and with pure revivals of religion, one of its first effects would be found in a return to those simple gospel truths, which were once acknowledged and prized, but are now neglected and scarcely understood. Should it please him, on the other hand, to awaken a general and interested attention to these heaven-descended truths, this would prove an auspicious omen that religion itself would rise from its depressions, and richly diffuse around us its sacred and saving influences.

The worthy and respected Author of this pamphlet has executed a task of no common importance. He has presented to the churches a view of the Theology of New England as it now exists, together with the means and steps by which it has arrived at its present position. The whole work is marked with great care and accuracy of investigation, with great clearness of statement, and with a candor which is mingled with a decided and warm attachment to the pure principles of gospel truth. In a work involving such extensiveness of general survey, and such a minute statement of particulars, it would be strange indeed, were there to be found no mistakes. In the present case, it is believed there are few, and those of small importance.

Mr. Wallace has laid our New England churches under great obligations. These obligations they will not be slow to acknowledge, or to appreciate. His pamphlet, it is anticipated, will excite a general attention. His statement will confirm the friends of truth, and will furnish matter of useful reflection to inquirers and errorists.

The writer of this Introduction is aware that, by his present and former communications to the public, he may incur the suspicion of severity towards his christian and ministerial brethren. But he pleads innocence. On this point, he can appeal to his own conscience, and he hopes also to his omniscient Judge. At no period has he felt more anxious to live and die in peace with every human being. Yet feeling that his final account is near, he is anxious to spend his last breath in defending the truth of God, and in opposing the errors which threaten its subversion. Conscious that he is liable to error, he knows that the same liability attends his valued brethren who differ from him in judgment. Nor is it impossible, that when he shall have retired from the stage, they may remember his warnings, with regret that they have not been regarded.

The Theology of New England is obviously in a state of transition. What is the point at which it will stop, is known only to Him who knows all things, and who loves his church with an affection far superior to that of the best of its friends. One thing is certain. Our spiritual condition will soon become either materially better, or materially worse. At such a time, there are reasons enough for fear and trembling, for sleepless vigilance, and active exertion; but none for despair, nor even for despondency. He who sways the sceptre of the world, sways likewise the sceptre of the Church. She cannot be swallowed and lost in the ocean, for her great Pilot is at the helm. Let Christians shake off their guilty slumbers; let them stand in their lot; let them rouse every nerve and sinew to active exertion, and all will yet be well. "GOD IS OUR REFUGE AND STRENGTH, A VERY PRESENT HELP IN TROUBLE." THEREFORE WILL NOT WE FEAR, THOUGH THE EARTH BE REMOVED, AND THOUGH THE MOUNTAINS BE CARRIED INTO THE MIDST OF THE SEA.

DANIEL DANA.

Newburyport, Nov. 19, 1855.

THE THEOLOGY OF NEW ENGLAND.

"THE Theology of New England," say the Editors of the Boston Congregationalist, "is not one simple, well-defined system. There has existed as great a variety among the New England divines, who are essentially orthodox, as among the divines of any other nation."* This fact renders it very difficult to point out, clearly and definitely, the principles commonly included under that term. There is no generally received creed, which embraces and authoritatively exhibits this theology. We must look for it in works on divinity usually regarded as standard, in labored articles of reviews, newspaper editorials, decisions of councils, published sermons, confessions of faith, and such other quarters as we may obtain light on the principles actually received and taught in the New England churches. From such sources as these

*March 15, 1850. The responsible editors of the "Congregationalist" at this date were Rev. E. Beecher, D. D., Rev. R. S. Storrs, D. D., and Rev. H. M. Dexter. The articles from which we quote were, it is believed, written by the then senior editor, Dr. Beecher.

the material for the following pages has been drawn. The reader must determine for himself the degree of credit to be attached to the several witnesses whose testimony is here recorded.

What the "Theology of New England"[*] at present is, may be inferred, with some degree of correctness from the influences which operated in forming it.

Hopkins, holding that all sin consists in selfish exercises, denying that there is in man any nature or tendency to sin that can be properly called sinful, exalting his doctrine of disinterested benevolence to being in general to the skies, rejecting the imputation of Adam's sin, teaching the doctrines of the atonement and justification in a loose and unsatisfactory manner, as well as deviating from the old faith in other important particulars, exerted a wide-spread and powerful influence on the ministry and churches in succeeding generations. Dr. Jonathan Edwards, who rejected the doctrine of imputation in all its branches, and who is regarded as the father of the new scheme of the atonement, which denied that Christ paid the debt his people owe to God, or died in their room and stead, or in any proper sense satisfied divine justice in their behalf, or secured any thing for them, or did any thing more than open up the way by which God can pardon and save sinners and still maintain the integrity of his government, and which claims that his death has the same favorable aspect on all men, is regarded by many as second only to his father. Long ago he was admitted into the catalogue of New England saints. Emmons, the great apostle of the "Exercise Scheme," who taught that there is no such thing as original sin, that there is no disposition to sin antecedent to unholy exercises, that all sin consists in exercises, that Christ merited nothing for sinners, that Christ by his death only opened up the way by which God might save all men, or none, as he saw fit, that justification signifies pardon of sin—no more, no less—that eternal life is bestowed as the reward of the believer's own sincere obedience, and who rejected imputation in every sense of the term, claiming that the distinction of Christ's obedience into active and passive is wholly unscriptural, instructed nearly a hundred students of theology, most of whom are now New England pastors, many of them occupying positions of great influence. Emmons held views respecting divine agency now accepted by few. These, however, are among his "aberrations in the direction of ultra Calvinism." Dr. Dwight, for many years President of Yale College, and Professor of Theology, while he taught fully and distinctly the old doctrine in relation to sin, depravity, and regeneration, nevertheless held views on imputation, the atonement, justification, and other subjects, nearly akin to those of Emmons, and palpably diverse from the theology of the Westminster standards. For a quarter of a century, Dr. Taylor and his colleagues, at New Haven, have been teaching that God could not prevent the entrance of sin into our system; he could not govern the world, so as to have less sin and less misery in it; he does the most and best he can to banish sin and bring in holiness; men persevere in sin in spite of all he can do to reclaim them; he converts and saves as many souls as he can, and would willingly save all if he could; there is no sinful nature antecedent to sinful acts or exercises; sin is the free preference of the world and worldly good to the will and glory of God; infants come into the world as free from sin as Adam; death no more proves sin in infants than in animals; the imputation of Adam's sin is unreasonable and absurd; regeneration is a change in the governing purpose of the mind; it is a gradual, progressive work; there is no change in the nature or disposition of the sinner antecedent to the exercise of right affections; the sinner may so resist the grace of God as to render it impossible for God to convert him; the agency of the Spirit in regeneration is altogether persuasive exerted through the medium of truth or motives; self-love or desire of happiness, is the primary cause or reason of all acts of preference or choice which fix supremely on any object. According to the Congregationalist, "Dr. Taylor has, within the last twenty years, instructed a larger number of students in the department of doctrinal theology than any other theological teacher in New England. These students are now, to a very considerable extent, the settled pastors in the churches of Massachusetts and Connecticut." "Besides, it is a well known fact, that a very large proportion of the pastors of New England who did not study theology under Dr. Taylor, hold essentially his views on the great and prominent doctrines of the gospel, and rank themselves as New School men."* Dr. Woods, for thirty-eight years Professor of Christian Theology at Andover, orthodox as he was, and Old School as he is now regarded, was understood to teach a system which might be considered a compromise between old Calvinism and Hopkinsianism. For near a quarter of a century, those memorable sentences, in his "Letters to Unitarians," in which he declared that the orthodox in New England, cannot with good conscience subscribe to every expression the Assembly's Catechism contains in relation to the doctrine of original sin, and that they cannot admit that the sinfulness of our natural fallen state consists in any measure in the guilt of Adam's first sin, remained unaltered as the record of his deliberate judgment.† It was not until advanced in life that he publicly announced his change of opinion in relation to the propriety of conforming to old school divines, in the use of theological terms. Throughout his entire connection with the Seminary, Professor Stuart, and during a part of it, Professor Park, were associated with him. Their influence, it

* Aug. 2, 1850. † Letters to Unitarians, p. 44, 1820.

may well be believed, did not, in any degree, remedy the deficiencies in his orthodoxy. Indeed, Dr. Dana complains that the instructions of Dr. Woods, because of opposing influences, had not been permitted to operate with full force on the minds of the students. There were collisions even in the pulpit of the Seminary.*

Such were some of the influences that operated in forming the prevailing theology of New England. What then is it?

Dr. Enoch Pond, Professor in the Theological Seminary at Bangor, Maine, one of the most eminent of New England divines, speaking of the union between the old Calvinists and Hopkinsians, in founding the Seminary at Andover, and in other benevolent enterprises, says:—"As they had now become a united body, they needed some name or phrase by which their theology might be designated. It was not Calvinism or Hopkinsianism, in the sense in which these terms had been used for half a century, but the coalition, the running together of both; and it is just here that we find the origin of a phrase about which there is no little dispute at the present day—THE NEW ENGLAND THEOLOGY."

Old Calvinism, though the prevailing theology in this section for the first one hundred and thirty years, could not, he argues, with any propriety be called New England theology, as it was not pecu-

* Dana's Remonstrance, p. 7

liar to New England. Hopkinsianism, he farther claims, never prevailed to such an extent as to be entitled to the name of New England theology. "But when," he says, "the great body of the Hopkinsians and Calvinists came to unite their forces to sustain the same institutions and publications, the result was a modified theology—neither old Calvinism, on the one hand, nor High Hopkinsianism on the other—which began to be called New England theology, and has been so designated ever since." "As the two classes which united in 1808, did not become perfectly one in sentiment, so the theology which they inculcated admitted of some diversity of statement and explanation. Still they were agreed in almost all important points, and wherein they differed they were pledged to mutual toleration. They unitedly held what have ever been considered the prominent points of Calvinism: such as the universal and unconditional purposes of God; the free moral agency of man; the entire sinfulness of the natural heart, in consequence of the original apostacy; the necessity of regeneration by the Spirit; justification by faith; redemption by the blood of Christ; the perseverance of saints unto eternal life; and the endless punishment of those who die in their sins. If these are Calvinistic doctrines, some of them peculiarly so, the New England theology is Calvinistic, and our ministers may with propriety be denominated Calvinists, still, they are not Calvinists in the exact sense of the

New England fathers a hundred years ago." Noticing a few particulars in which the current theology of New England differs from the Calvinism of a former age, he mentions the imputation of Adam's sin, inability, directions to the unconverted, regeneration, and the atonement. He says, moreover, that New England divines are not agreed among themselves, but differ as to the nature of sin, our connection with Adam, regeneration, and kindred doctrines. These differences, he claims, are found among the soundest and most orthodox theologians, and therefore ought to be no bar to union and coöperation. Such are the views of this theology held by one of its ablest and most sober-minded advocates.*

Professor Park, of Andover, is, however, the most devoted admirer, as well as the ablest expounder of this system. His statements have, therefore, peculiar authority. In the closing article of his late controversy with Professor Hodge, of Princeton, he thus writes:—"We beg leave, therefore, first of all, to explain the term New England theology. It signifies the formal creed which a majority of the most eminent theologians in New England have explicitly or implicitly sanctioned, during and since the time of Edwards. It includes not the peculiarities in which Edwards differed, as he is known to have differed from the larger part of his most eminent followers, nor the

*Sketch of the Theological Hist. of New England. Boston Cong., Nos. 7 and 8.

peculiarities in which any one of his followers differed, as some of them did, from the larger part of the others; but it comprehends the principles, with their logical sequences, which the greater number of our most celebrated divines have approved expressly, or by implication. It was first called New-light Divinity, then New Divinity, afterward Edwardean, more recently Hopkintonian or Hopkinsian. From the fact that Edwards, Hopkins, West, and Catlin, resided in Berkshire county, it was once called Berkshire divinity. When it was embraced by Andrew Fuller, Dr. Ryland, Robert Hall, Sutcliffe, Carey, Jay, and Erskine, it was called American theology by the English, in order to discriminate it from the European systems.* It has been denominated New England theology, in order to distinguish it from the systems that have prevailed in other parts of the land. In 1756, two years before the death of Edwards, there were, according to Dr. Hopkins, not more than four or five clergymen who espoused this new theology. In 1773, it was advocated by about forty-five ministers; and Dr. Hopkins says that in 1796 it was favored by somewhat more than a hundred. In 1787, Dr. Stiles men-

* In relation to the above assertion, an eminent old school Professor of Theology uses the following language: "Professor Park's assertion, that Hopkinsianism was embraced by Fuller, Ryland, Hall, Erskine, etc., is so unfounded, and can be proved to be so by the writings of the persons named, that I am surprised at its rashness. The distinction between moral and natural ability—which, however, is far older than Edwards—and the unlimited extent, or rather the boundless efficacy of the Atonement, are the only ideas which they derive from New England."

tions as among its champions the two Edwardses, Bellamy, Hopkins, Trumbull, Smalley, Judson, Spring, Robinson, Strong, Dwight, Emmons. In 1799 Hopkins appended the names of West, Levi Hart, Backus, Presidents Balch and Fitch. We may now add such honored men as Dr. Catlin, President Appleton, Dr. Austin. They gave form and pressure to our theological system. They were imperfect men. They did not harmonize on every theme; but a decided majority of them stood firm for the three radical principles, that sin consists in choice, that our natural power equals, and that it limits our duty."

Characterizing this system particularly, he says: "It is marked by certain new features." He does not specify them, but says in general: "We do not mean to say that the Edwardean school discovered principles that were never thought of before. They claim to have brought out into bold relief the obscurer faith of good men in all ages. They gave a new distinctness, a new prominence to doctrines which had been more vaguely believed by the church. They produced new arguments for a faith which had been speculatively opposed by men who had practically sanctioned it." As an example, he mentions the doctrine that "an entirely depraved man has a natural power to do all that is required of him," claiming "that it has been so clearly unfolded by New England divines that it properly belongs to their distinctive system." He further maintains that

"New England theology is Calvinism in an improved form." "It does not profess to be original in its cardinal truths. It has ever claimed that they are the common faith of the church; that they are recognised in many evangelical creeds; that Calvinism contains the substance of New England theology, not always well-proportioned, not seldom intermingled with the remnants of an erring scholasticism, and sometimes enveloped in inconsistencies, and expressed in a nervous style. The substance of our theology is Calvinistic: here it is old. Much of its self-consistency is Edwardean and Hopkinsian; here it is new. It is not mere Calvinism, but it is consistent Calvinism. It is a revised and corrected edition of the Genevan creed." As specimens of the crooked parts of Calvinism that New England divines have straightened out, he mentions the agency of God in producing sin, and the nature of necessity. "Strong, practical common sense," he says, "is another characteristic of the New England divinity." This feature he illustrates by a reference to its theory concerning the nature of moral evil, affirming that all sin consists in sinful acts, or exercises, and denying that there is any antecedent sinful nature. In his remarks on this topic it is a noticeable fact, that Prof. Park has the hardihood to claim Pres. Edwards and Dr. Dwight as holding this theory. Does the learned Professor suppose that his readers are not capable of comprehending for themselves the plainest and most direct statements of these divines? In the next place, he characterizes "New Englaud theology as a comprehensive system of biblical science." "It unites a high, but not an ultra Calvinism, on the decrees and agency of God, with a philosophical, but not an Arminian theory, on the freedom and worth of the human soul." "When its opposers think of its efforts to justify the ways of God to man, they hastily accuse it of Arminianism; and when they turn their minds to its descriptions of the supreme, universal Governor, they hastily accuse it of hyper-Calvinism." In the last place, he claims that "it is the only system of speculative orthodoxy that can endure examination, and therefore destined to prevail." "It is a system which will bear to be looked at, and is not a theology of mere 'dissolving views.' The science of the world is in favor of it. The moral instincts of the race are in favor of it. The common sense of common men is in favor of it. They can be kept back from it only by the incessant roll of a polemic drum, which alarms them by its discordant sounds." This synopsis of Prof. Park's article will show the light in which this system is regarded by its great champion. A shade of difference will be observed between him and Prof. Pond.*

Still another eminent divine has undertaken to interpret the phrase "New England theology." We refer to Dr. Woods. A short time before his

* Bibliotheca Sacra, January, 1852.

death he published a pamphlet, in which he maintained that the theology of New England is simply that of the Shorter Catechism—nothing more—nothing less—nothing different. All who swerve from it, he maintains, swerve from the true New England theology. He is, however, compelled to admit that among those who would be numbered with orthodox ministers, there are individuals who entertain opinions obviously at variance with what he calls the settled theology of the Puritans. These erroneous doctrines are, that the purpose of God to save sinners rests wholly on his foreknowledge of their repentance, faith, and obedience—that Adam's posterity begin their existence, as he did, free from moral corruption or any sinful propensity—that God was not able to exclude sin from a world of free moral agents, however much he may have desired it—that when God has favored sinners with the privileges of the gospel and the strivings of the Spirit, he has done all he can for their conversion—that the new birth consists in a right exercise of free agency—that Christ did not die in place of sinners, but merely made an affecting demonstration of God's readiness to save sinners, etc. These opinions he looked upon as exceptions to the common belief. He was persuaded that the great body of Congregational ministers and churches are sound in the faith.* Here, however, the editors of the Congregation-

* Theology of the Puritans, pp. 39-42.

alist joined issue with the doctor, and maintained that the prevalent theology of New England is not in all respects that of the Catechism, but something very different.* Prof. Pond, while he admits that Old School Calvinism was the prevailing theology in New England for the first one hundred and thirty years, insists that since that time it has come to be something different.† The editors of the Panoplist—a periodical started in Boston, January, 1850, for the express purpose of counteracting the erroneous influences abroad, but which, after a sickly existence of not quite three years, was discontinued for want of support, say: "We think the charity of Dr. Woods has led him to a more hopeful view of the state of the orthodox faith than the facts will warrant. We have no doubt the defection, both in Puritan habits and doctrine, is far more extensive than is generally believed, or even suspected."‡ High authorities among both new and old school men, it will thus be seen, differ from Dr. Woods, in their estimate of New England theology. Men, however, whose judgment is worthy of very high respect substantially agree with him, as will appear in the sequel.

The editors of the Panoplist, in their introductory address, give a more formal expression of their estimate of the new theology. They repre-

* Congregationalist for 1850 and 1851.

† Sketches of the Theological History of New England, Nos. 7 and 8.

‡ Panoplist, Vol. III, p. 104.

sent it as having carried away "a great portion of the Congregational churches." Styling it a "species of rationalism," they use the following language:—"We have said it is dangerous in the last degree. But we have not been beating the air, telling a story of a chimera, or some frightful object which every body has heard of but nobody seen. We speak of it as something which exists, which exists among us, which is fast spreading itself among our churches. We speak what we know, and testify of something which we have seen. We know that it has long shown its influence in our colleges, that it characterises the discussions in our theological seminaries and the discourses of the pulpit: we know that it is rapidly extending itself, and threatens a very general defection from the faith of our fathers." Let it be observed that reference is here made to the inroad of principles different from, and what we would call still more erroneous than the New England orthodoxy of a quarter of a century ago.*

Prof. Hodge of Princeton, in the concluding article of his controversy with Prof. Park, has given us a glimpse of what he regards as New England theology. His views are exhibited in the following extract. It will be seen that he agrees very nearly with Dr. Woods:—"There is another feature in Prof. Park's mode of conducting this discussion, which is very little to our taste. He con-

* Panoplist, Vol. I, p. 9.

stantly endeavors to represent us as assailing New England theology. This is a *ruse de guerre* every way unworthy of a candid disputant. We stated, as the three radical principles of the Anti-Agustinian system—'First, all sin consists in sinning; that there can be no moral character but in moral acts; secondly, that the power to the contrary is essential to free agency; that a free agent may always act contrary to any influence, not destructive of his freedom, that may be brought to bear upon him; thirdly, that ability limits responsibility; that men are responsible only so far as they have adequate power to do what is required of them, or that they are responsible for nothing not under the control of the will.' If there is one characteristic of New England theology more prominent than any other, it is opposition to these principles. The world-wide fame of President Edwards, as a theologian, rests mainly on his thorough refutation of them. In this opposition, Bellamy, Dwight, and the other great men of New England, were no less strenuous than Edwards. The aberration of the advocates of the 'Exercise Scheme,' though it led them to a denial of at least the first of the above principles, was in the direction of ultra Calvinism. It was not until the rise of what is popularly called New Havenism, that those principles were rejected by any other class of New England divines reputed orthodox. It is Prof. Park and not we who is the assailant of New England theology, a fact which he will not be able to conceal. We recently heard of a certain Unitarian gentleman who seemed honestly to believe that Trinitarianism is dying out in this country. It is possible that a similar hallucination may lead Prof. Park to regard the little coterie to which he belongs as all New England."* Such is the estimate of the great living champion of the old school theology.

After the controversy between Prof. Park of Andover, and Prof. Hodge of Princeton, closed, in 1852, Dr. Lord, President of Dartmouth College, published a letter to Dr. Dana of Newburyport. In it he thus speaks of the theology of New England:—"Prof. Hodge, Dr. Woods, and others, of the Edwardean school in New England, have good hopes. They imagine that Calvinism is still ascendant among the churches of the fathers. *But I fear they err.* I fear that Prof. Park judges truly that the current of theological opinion is running in the 'new' channels. I fear he would be found, if occasion should serve, in the centre of a larger 'coterie' than these good men imagine. For IT IS TRUE *that the Assembly's Catechism has mostly ceased from the families, schools, and churches of New England. It is true that wanton hands have marred that venerable digest itself, and few care to wipe the infamy away. It is true that we are altering our confessions and covenants, our psalms and hymns, and our style of worship in gen-*

*Princeton Review, Vol. XXIII, p. 693-4.

eral, to suit a more highly illuminated state of the public mind. Unequivocal signs exist that a great change is coming over New England. And there is plenary evidence that this change is referable to a period when our theology was diverted into a speculative channel, when its learned teachers began to light their torch at the altar of the imaginative reason, and, in their circuits after divine knowledge, went up to Alexandria and Athens, rather than to Jerusalem."*

After showing, at considerable length, that the theology of New England was the theology set forth in the Catechism, he uses the following language:—" The Professor, if he pleases, in his commendable, though misdirected zeal of knowledge, may cull the flowers of the patristic metaphysics, and distil them in his well furnished laboratory at Andover. He may digest these essences, if he will, in his concentrated eclectic solvent. He may give out the compound, if he will, as a panacea for the moral and theological diseases of the age, and multiply certificates of its healing power over the catholicons that have gone before it; but let it not be labelled 'New England theology.' That endures no counterfeit. It has a regular Puritan image and superscription, unique, intelligible and unmistakeable, to the end of time. A spurious article may supplant it, and have its run till overtaken by some more sublimated spe-

* Letter, p. 27.

cific. But it cannot be long mistaken for the genuine. We have seen many attempts to give currency to the false by the alleged authority of venerated names. But they have always failed. Whoever calls Taylorism New England theology now; or imagines that it could have sprung from the heart of Edwards, or even from his head, except in sleep? The modern digests of the ancient incoherent and equivocal speculations, may, indeed, become New England theology, if it is right to call them by that sacred name. I fear they will; for the majority would rather be killed by nostrums, than cured by the regular physicians. Such has ever been the history of sophistry and unbelief, and we have no right to expect exemption from a universal law. But these specifics can never be New England theology—*as it was.* They can never stand the reaction of the Assembly's Catechism, or the Statutes at Andover. God be thanked! we have made sure of something in New England. The Puritans did not bleed and die for a chimera."*

Thus writes an eminent divine who occupies a place on one of New England's watch towers. His testimony is worthy of special attention.

The next witness, whose testimony we would add to the foregoing, is from a different class—embracing but very few individuals, yet well qualified to testify in such a case—New England

* Letter, p. 33–4.

Presbyterians. On fast day, 1848, Rev. W. W. Eells, pastor of the Second Presbyterian Church in Newburyport, in connection with the General Assembly, himself a New England man, perfectly familiar with the prevalent theology, preached two sermons, specially intended to point out the defections of the descendants of the Puritans from the faith and practice of their fathers. These sermons were afterwards published. The author talks plainly—bluntly, indeed. Take the following extracts, as exhibiting his estimate of New England theology:—"Notwithsanding the cry of Puritan theology from pulpits, and tracts, and pamphlets, and newspapers, and more aspiring periodicals, it is evident from our practice, *that there is very little of true Puritan theology amongst us.*" "*It is an undeniable fact*, that very little doctrinal preaching of any kind is found in the pulpits of the present day, in this land of the Puritans. A sickly sentimentalism—a morality scarcely more refined than that of Plato—the discussion of abstract topics of speculation—the advocacy of some scheme of real benevolence, or of the multitude, whose name is legion, of counterfeit schemes of good—or, at most, the indefinite and indirect preaching *about* the gospel, the delicate and distant allusion to some of the plainer first principles of truth—this is the provision now too generally set before the sons of those who desired to be fed, and were fed, and sustained, and strengthened on the strong meat of the gospel of grace. This is a truth—an awful truth. And many an humble Christian has mourned over it when he has gone to the sanctuary and found no Savior there; and out of a heart burdened with grief, has groaned with Mary—'They have taken away my Lord, and I know not where they have laid him.'" "The popular theology of the day—that which is held to an alarming extent, and is increasing, almost unrebuked, and which bids fair soon to be universal—is a direct contradiction, in every important point, to the theology and doctrine of our fathers." "The adherents of this new system of antiquated error and falsehood, commence their work by sinking away this foundation stone," (the doctrine of original sin.) "Sin," they say, "is voluntary action in view of known law. Sin is altogether action. The very idea of a sinful disposition, a depraved nature, a sinful propensity, is scouted and ridiculed as an absurdity." "The representative character of Adam, as well as any imputation of his sin, or any thing like inherent sinfulness or hereditary depravity, is utterly denied and derided." "I but echo the cry of these new system-mongers when I say that this doctrine of atonement, and this doctrine of justification," (that taught in the Confession and Catechisms,) "are almost wholly unknown among the descendants of the Puritans in this land of their prayers. And not only so, but men in high places in the church seem to find a malignant pleasure, first in caricaturing these doctrines, and then in holding them up to derision and contempt." After describing the doctrine of the Confession as to the application of redemption, he goes on to say:—"But all this glorious truth is a fable, and a dream, to these wise men—wise in old folly." "Regeneration is a change from sinful action to holy action. And this man, who is thus to change, is not dead in sins. He is as fully able to keep all the law of God as Adam was." "All the work of the Spirit is reduced to mere persuasion, to the application of motives to the will of man. He may bring the truth home with power upon the understanding, but he cannot change the heart." Mr. Eells closes up this discussion with the following energetic language: "Here I will pause, not that the catalogue of falsehood and of folly is exhausted, but that enough has been said to show that all the foundations of Puritan theology are overthrown by those who vainly boast that the Puritans are their fathers. These are the doctrines that are taught by professors of theology, that are preached from the pulpit in this land of the pilgrims. And the evil is wide-spread, and is fast extending itself. THIS IS AN UNDENIABLE TRUTH." Thus a New England Presbyterian characterizes the prevalent theology.

The author of the "Andover Fuss"—a pamphlet published in 1853, in review of Dr. Dana's remonstrance, we would bring forward as another witness. The pamphlet, though anonymous, yet bears marks of being "by authority." Speaking of the efforts of the few genuine Old School men in this region, the writer says:—" They have compassed sea and land to proselyte New England to a faith which it abhors, and which it shook off as offensive to the first principles of justice and the most rooted convictions of common sense. Those cast-off errors, for which the orthodox *would not be held responsible*, it requires no gift of prophecy to foretell, *will never regain their ascendancy over New England*, or ever come out, *barefaced*, in many, if in any of her churches; the Westminster doctrine of original sin will never come back to the region from which it has been so decisively and considerately cast out. We only wonder that men of so much wisdom should be men of so much folly. If the triple force of cunning, secrecy, and combination, could insure success, theirs would not be doubtful. What arts have been spared to deluge the orthodox churches of New England with a *scholastic catechism, which it is hard to understand, and still harder to believe?* What manœuvres have been wanting to lay hold of every religious press, and turn its weeklies and quarterlies up the channel of time? What subtle scheming and patient assiduity have not attested the fond desire and fixed intent to overturn the platform of Congregationalism, and foist into its place a system of disguised, but rank Presbyterianism? What inventions have not been plied to coerce the elder theological seminaries in New England to caress a doctrine, which, in 1820, was branded by Dr. Woods as a fugitive and a vagabond, or else to direct theological students to a seminary that was an Ishmaelite from its conception. What secret correspondence has not been carried on to extend over New England an ultraism of orthodoxy, which that region had lost sight of? What espionage has not leered at a freedom of thought that ranged over a field *broader than the dogmas of Westminster*, or *indulged in a moral sentiment at variance with its obsolete and preposterous doctrine of original sin?* What vigilance has not been on the look out for vacant pulpits, agencies, and offices of honor and influence in seminaries of learning, to manage into them candidates of stockstill fixedness in an *effete* creed, and to fly-blow such as ventured a step out of the magic circle of the Westminster faith?"

Desiring to throw light from every quarter on this subject we present two more extracts. An article in the Boston Congregationalist of Aug. 2d, 1850, understood to be from the pen of Dr. Edward Beecher, who twenty years ago was regarded as a "strenuous advocate of Taylorism," contains the following language:—"We should like to know, however, what is to be allowed hereafter to pass for orthodoxy in Massachusetts and Connecticut. Within the last twenty years Dr. Taylor has, we suppose, instructed a larger number of students in the department of doctrinal theology than any other theological teacher in New England. These students are now, to a considerable extent, the settled pastors in the churches of Massachusetts and Connecticut. . . . But besides, it is a well-known fact, that a very large proportion of the pastors of New England who did not study theology under Dr. Taylor, hold essentially his views on the great and prominent doctrines of the gospel, and rank themselves as New School men. These views were entertained by multitudes long before Dr. Taylor's day. We have been interested of late in noticing how this matter works. Our delegate to the Old School General Assembly is very happy to inform that venerable body that the orthodoxy of Massachusetts was never in a more healthy, vigorous, and prosperous state. True, unquestionably. But if nothing is to be reckoned as orthodoxy in Massachusetts but *Old School* Calvinism, the delegate ought not to have made any such report. He ought frankly to have told that body that Massachusetts' orthodoxy was sadly on the decline. It seems to us, our Old School friends, when they make a *summing up* of the condition of orthodoxy, are very glad to reckon in all the New School men, because they would make rather a meagre show without us; but in other circumstances they magisterially talk about our having embraced 'some form of rationalism.'"

The last general estimate of the Theology of New England, which we would present, is that made by Rev. William T. Dwight, D. D., of Portland, Maine, in a discourse delivered in Boston before the "Congregational Board of Publication,"

May 30, 1855. His theme was "Characteristics of New England Theology." He described it as independent, steadily progressive, truly scriptural, and as having formed the New England character. Speaking of it as scriptural he uses the following language:

"When we would thus describe the theology of New England, we intend that it is more scriptural than the Apostle's Creed, or than the Nicene Creed; than the theology of Luther and Melancthon, of Knapp and Tholuck and Hengstenberg; than the theology of Leighton, of Butler, and Magee, or than the piebald theology of Coleridge; than that of Symington and Chalmers; or than that of Calvin and Turretin. Or, if such comparisons are thought to savor of presumption, it is intended that this theology would peculiarly harmonize with such a system of divine truth as the great Apostle to the Gentiles would have prepared soon after completing his Epistle to the Romans, had he been then led to undertake such a work, and without the immediate guidance of inspiration in its execution."

In presenting these testimonies, we have had no pre-conceived theory of our own to make good. Our aim has been simply to throw light on the subject from all quarters, to aid the reader in forming a correct estimate of the real facts.

We now proceed to point out the views of the great facts in the plan of salvation prevalent in the Puritan churches of New England. At the

Synod, met in Boston, A. D. 1680, composed of ministers and messengers from all the New England churches, according to Cotton Mather, "the Confession of Faith, consented to by the Congregational churches of England in a synod met at the Savoy—which, excepting a few variations, was the same with what was agreed by the Reverend Assembly at Westminster, and afterwards by the General Assembly of Scotland—was twice publicly read, examined, and approved, and some small variations made from that of the Savoy, in compliance with that of the Westminster, and so, after such collations, but no contentions, voted and printed as the faith of New England."* We have examined this Confession with care. As far as its exhibition of the plan of redemption is concerned, it corresponds in every particular with that of the Westminster divines. In the most important chapters, there is not even a verbal difference. Such was the standard of ancient orthodoxy in New England. We shall aim, in the sequel, to point out whatever important departures from it have taken place. We shall be careful to set down as true only well established facts.

Orthodox Congregationalists are usually spoken of as divided into Old and New School. The position of these parties is clearly stated in the following extract from the "Boston Congregationalist," of September 13, 1850:—" Those who con-

* Magnolia, Vol. II: p. 156.

sistently hold and unfold the views of Edwards, in his treatise 'on Virtue,' are *New School* divines, though their more proper name is *New England* divines. Those who repudiate these as false and dangerous, are *Old School*." In answer to the question, Who are to be ranked among the Old School? the writer says:—"The Princeton divines, the editors of the modern Panoplist, and all who with them wish to revolutionize the theology of New England." Again, in answer to the inquiry, Would he include the Calvinists of New England, as distinguished from the Hopkinsians, among the Old School? he says:—"By no means. They are separated by an impassable gulf from Old School Princeton divines. For what the Princetonians abhor and renounce as the source and fountain of all evil, the old Calvinists of New England have eminently honored as the truth of God." It is well to remember, that in the judgment of the editors of the Congregationalist, those divines in New England known as "Old Calvinists," are separated in sentiment by an impassable gulf from the Princeton divines. Even among the New School or New England divines, as the Congregationalist prefers to style them, there is a well-defined line of division. Of these, one class is sometimes called Old School, and the other New. The former is, in their judgment, but a "meagre party." In the sequel the theology of these parties will be carefully distinguished.

I. *Inspiration of the Scriptures.*

Among those who claim to be included within the pale of orthodoxy, are some—how many we have no means of knowing—who reject, or at least practically deny, the commonly received doctrine of inspiration. Dr. Woods, who is very solicitous to vindicate the orthodoxy of the orthodox, is compelled to acknowledge "that lax opinions are occasionally put forth as to the inspiration of the Scriptures." He goes on to say:—"Some ministers, who wish to be called orthodox, show more confidence in their own reason than in the holy Scriptures. They set aside, or new-model those teachings of revelation which transcend their own intellectual powers, and which require them to submit their understanding to the absolute authority of the Word of God."* If the writer is not misinformed, at least one instance has occurred of a council ordaining and installing a man, who, when examined, avowed his disbelief of the plenary inspiration of the Scriptures. These views must, however, be regarded as exceptional to those generally prevalent.

II. *Election.*

On this subject "The Confession of Faith" teaches that "Those of mankind who are predes-

* Theology of the Puritans, p. 12.

tinated unto life, God hath chosen in Christ unto everlasting glory, out of his mere free grace and love, without any foresight of faith or good works, or perseverance in either of them, or any thing in the creature as conditions or causes moving him thereunto." It also affirms that the "means are foreordained," and that "all the elect are effectually called unto faith by the Spirit, justified, adopted, sanctified, and kept through faith unto salvation."* This is the doctrine of all who have any claim to be regarded as Calvinists. Dr. Woods, however, acknowledges that there are among those who claim to be regarded as orthodox, some who hold the "Arminian view of the doctrine of election, namely, that the purpose of God to save sinners rests wholly upon his foreknowledge of their repentance, faith, and obedience." How many hold these views it is difficult to ascertain. It is, however, believed to be a fact that "orthodox" ministers very generally, if not universally, exchange, on equal terms, with avowed Arminians. It is also believed to be a fact, that there is little, or no appreciable difference, as to the principles they ordinarily preach. Yet the formal creed of the mass of "orthodox" ministers is doubtless Calvinistic, as contradistinguished from Arminianism.

* Confession of Faith, Chap. III, Sec. 5 and 6.

III. *Adam's Relation to his Posterity.*

On this subject the doctrine of the Westminster standards is, that "our first parents being the root of all mankind, the guilt of their first sin was imputed, and the same death in sin and corrupted nature conveyed to all their posterity descending from them by ordinary generation."*—"The covenant being made with Adam as a public person, not for himself but for his posterity, all mankind descending from him * * * sinned in him and fell with him in that first transgression."†—"The sinfulness of that estate whereinto man fell consisteth," they say among other things, "in the guilt of Adam's first sin."‡—"We are by nature children of wrath, and justly liable to all punishments in this world and in that which is to come."‖ There are some among the orthodox who hold this doctrine. Among these, Dr. Woods, during the last years of his life at least, claimed to be numbered. In his lectures, as published, he vindicates what he understood to be the Westminster doctrine on this subject, as well as the propriety of using the phraseology employed in those standards. There is good reason to believe, however, that this is not the prevalent doctrine in New England. Dr. Woods, in his Letters to Unitarians, declared:—"*The imputation of Adam's sin*

* Confession of Faith, Chap. VI, Sec. 3. † L. Cat. Q. 23. ‡ L. Cat. Q. 25. ‖ L. Cat. Q. 27.

*to his posterity, in any sense which those words naturally and properly convey, is a doctrine which we do not believe.** The editors of the Congregationalist bear testimony to the correctness of this statement. They say, speaking of the above extract and its context—" It admirably sets forth the true position of New England divines."† The Doctrinal Book and Tract Society—an association organized for the express purpose of disseminating what its members regard as the truth, and in which all parties are united, in No. 2 of its Series of Tracts, says:—" Sin, as well as holiness, is strictly personal, and cannot be transferred from one to another. By this it is meant, that no sinful act of one person can ever become the sinful act of another person. Although fallen Adam's posterity are constituted sinners by means of their connection with him as their public head, yet *his* sin is not *their* sin. God declares—' The soul that sinneth, it shall die;' and, in connection with this, he teaches that no person shall bear the iniquity of another, but only his own; that no person shall be punished for the sin of another, but only for his own sin. Thus, it appears, that in consequence of the first offence of the first man, all his descendants have become sinners."‡

This language is introduced in such a connection that there is no doubt but that it was intended to state what is regarded as the truth in oppo-

*p. 44. †June 22, 1849. ‡p. 1 and 2.

sition to the ancient doctrine. Prof. Pond, after describing the old theology on this subject says:—"I think there are few clergymen in New England now, who would explain the connection of our sin with that of Adam in this way."* Professor Park's theory has no place for this doctrine: indeed it seems to be absolutely inconsistent with it. Prof. Stuart, with much learning and ingenuity combated the doctrines of Adam's Federal Headship and the imputation of his sin. He teaches "that all of Adam's posterity are affected by his offence, and have sustained great losses thereby, and are subjected to many evils." "But this," he claims, "is something very different from proper *punishment.* The fall of Adam brought our race into a new state of probation. The whole race are now heirs by nature of a frail and dying condition; they are no longer in that state in which they are inclined to holiness. And this comes on all without any concurrence of their own. But this may still be regarded in another light than that of simple punishment. It is trial: it is discipline: it is probation *sui generis.*"† The Old School doctrine, Dr. Taylor rejected with indignation. "To believe this," he exclaims, "I must renounce the reason God has given me; I must believe it also in the face of the oath of God to its falsehood entered on the record."‡ Dr. Dwight does not teach Adam's federal headship; he argues that

* Sketches of N. E. Theology, No. 8. † Stuart on the Romans, p. 595.
‡ Concio ad clerum.

the posterity of Adam are neither guilty of his transgression nor punished for it: the simple proposition, "that in consequence of the apostacy of Adam all men have sinned," embodies his whole doctrine on the subject.* Emmons and Hopkins both discarded the Westminster doctrine. This is well known. It may therefore be affirmed with all confidence, that the doctrine of Adam's federal headship and the imputation of his sin, is not a doctrine of the theology prevailing in New England. Some think that the New England doctrine differs from the Westminster doctrine on this subject only in the language employed to express it. We think differently. The two doctrines seem to us palpably diverse. Hopkins, Emmons, Dwight, Taylor, Stuart, and others were certainly able to comprehend the meaning of terms; and beyond all doubt they rejected not merely what they considered objectionable phraseology but also a well-defined principle, which they certainly well understood.

IV. *Sin and Depravity.*

On this subject the Confession of Faith teaches that our first parents being "the root of all mankind * * * the same death in sin and corrupted nature were conveyed to all their posterity, descending from them by ordinary generation." "This

* Sermon 32.

corruption of nature, both itself and all the motions thereof are truly and properly sin."* And the Shorter Catechism teaches that "the sinfulness of that state whereinto man fell consists in the guilt of Adam's first sin, the want of original righteousness, and the corruption of his whole nature, which is commonly called original sin, together with all actual transgressions which proceed from it."† "Sin is any want of conformity to or transgression of the law of God."‡

On this subject, New England divines differ. Some hold to the old doctrine of a sinful, corrupt, depraved nature in man, antecedent to all sinful acts. Such is the position of Dwight and Woods. They believe in original sin, as well as actual. Others, again, maintain that all sin consists in acts or exercises contrary to God's law, and that there is no such thing as a sinful nature or disposition antecedent to sinful exercises. These are pre-eminently the New School. In this fundamental principle, the regular Hopkinsians, New Haven divines, and Emmonites, all agree. The "Exercise" men, as they are called, however, differ among themselves. Some admit the existence of a propensity or disposition *to* sin, but deny that this propensity or disposition is at all sinful. Others refuse to admit that there is, in any man, any such bias, but maintain that all exercises of the soul are the direct result of the divine efficiency.

* Chap. vi: Sect. 3 and 5. † Q. 18. ‡ Q. 14.

The former call Hopkins father, the latter Emmons. The New Haven men plead that infants come into the world as free from sin as Adam, and that they are not subjects of moral government until they become moral agents. The advocates of this scheme, commonly known as the "Exercise Scheme," are neither few nor feeble. Taylor and his coadjutors were its avowed champions. Prof. Park, of Andover, in his "Convention Sermon," and in his controversy with Prof. Hodge growing out of it, boldly avowed and earnestly maintained there is no nature in man antecedent to sinful acts that can truly and properly be called sinful. "That all sin consists in action," Dr. Dana declares to be Prof. Park's favorite maxim.

These principles—which are throughout totally inconsistent with the old doctrine of original sin, which indeed cut it up root and branch—are believed to be widely prevalent. They have been long taught at New Haven and Andover—the leading orthodox theological seminaries in New England. They are asserted and defended by the most prominent and influential divines. The editors of the Panoplist, in their introductory address,* say:—"For the last fifteen or twenty years, the great doctrines of original sin and regeneration, as they were understood by the reformers and the churches of the Reformation, have been

* Vol. I, p. 12

assailed with the same arts, and for the most part with the same arguments and objections, which they encounter among Socinians and infidels." "The fundamental doctrine of the New School in theology is this; that there *is*, and *can* be nothing holy or sinful in any intelligent being aside from his acts; that all the inherent inclinations, dispositions, and affections of the soul, are innocent, neither holy nor sinful; that Adam came into this world without any inherent holiness, his moral excellence originating with himself, and his posterity come into life with no dispositions or inclinations morally wrong. This is also the fundamental principle of Pelagianism, which necessarily leads to all the rest, and can end only in gross rationalism, or infidelity, which has always been the issue of this doctrine. It was also the fundamental principle of New England Arminianism, whose developments have been Socinianism and Pantheism." This theology, they declare, has affected a "great portion of the Congregational churches." On these extracts the editors of the Congregationalist remark:—"Why limit the prevalence of this peculiar type of theology to the last fifteen or twenty years? Do not the editors know, that what is here denominated the fundamental principle of the New School theology, i. e., that all sin consists in action, has been very generally held in New England, and to a considerable extent out of it, for more than fifty years; that it was the theology of Hopkins and Emmons, of West and

Spring, and the men of that day—names great and venerable; that it was the *chief distinguishing feature* of that school and system, called, from its illustrious founder, the Hopkinsian; that it is the theology not only of some of the ablest and best men now living, but of the greatest and best names on the roll of American divines for the last half century; that it is the theology of the very men whose writings the Doctrinal Tract Society are engaged at this very time in publishing?"* When Mr. Finney was in Boston, something more than twenty years ago, he preached this "fundamental doctrine of the New School theology." His position was severely reviewed in a religious journal of that city. Something of a controversy followed. In a review of the whole subject, the "Spirit of the Pilgrims" says:—"*A vast majority* of the orthodox clergy of New England might be represented, on this ground, as denying the 'doctrine of entire depravity,' with the same propriety as Mr. Finney; for they agree with him in discarding the notion of a *sinful bias or taste*, as distinct from, and prior to, sinful exercises of the will."† Many of those among New England divines, who hold to the doctrine of an original, depraved nature, seem to regard those who maintain the "Exercise Scheme" as equally entitled with themselves to be styled "orthodox." Dr. Woods pleads a compromise. Dr. Pond speaks of "this

* Cong. Feb. 1, 1850. † Spirit of the Pilgrims, vol. v., p. 164.

difference as existing among our soundest theologians," and "as in practice amounting to very little." He says:—"It has proved no bar to fraternal union and coöperation, and expresses a hope that it may be so in time to come."* Prof. Park has for many years occupied the most important chair in the most important theological institution in New England. He has boldly taught this and kindred doctrines all along, and teaches them still. The venerable Dr. Dana, an eminent Old School divine, who has been a member of the board of trustees from the beginning, remonstrated more than five years ago. Little attention was given to his solemn words. All now seems quiet. The number of students at Andover has not apparently been diminished by this cause. Prof. Park is secure in his place. Now what do these facts tell? Simply this: *The orthodox sentiment in Massachusetts sustains the Professor of Christian Theology at Andover.* It is true that some—we might, perhaps, say many—do not approve his teachings on this subject. They lament the position of things and would gladly see it altered. Yet we cannot see how the conclusion can be avoided, that the popular voice endorses Prof. Park, or also agrees with Dr. Pond, in believing the difference between him and the Old School, to amount in practice to very little. A review of all the facts certainly justifies us in affirming that the doctrine of original

* Sketches, etc., viii.

native depravity is not a principle of the prevailing theology of New England.

V. *Human Inability.*

The doctrine of the Confession of Faith on this subject is expressed in the following terms:—" By this original corruption we are utterly indisposed, disabled, and made opposite to all good, and wholly inclined to all evil."*—" Man by his fall hath wholly lost all ability of will to any spiritual good accompanying salvation: so, as a natural man, being altogether averse from that good and dead in sin, is not able by his own strength, to convert himself or prepare himself thereunto."†—The Catechism says: " No mere man since the fall is able in this life perfectly to keep the commandments of God."‡ This plain and unequivocal language is regarded by Old School divines as an admirable exhibition of the doctrine of Scripture on this subject. Since the days of Edwards, however, theologians of all classes have been accustomed to speak of man as possessing full natural ability to keep God's law, but as destitute of moral ability—as naturally able, but morally unable to do God's bidding. This phraseology has been, and still is, employed in widely different senses. Under it one man teaches Scripture truth,

* Chap. vi: Sect. 4. † Chap. ix: Sect. 3. ‡ Quest. 82.

another soul-destroying error. The Old School man, wishing to employ the phraseology immortalized by the elder Edwards, *concedes* man's natural ability—understanding thereby those powers and faculties necessary to constitute a moral agent. At the same time he asserts strongly man's moral inability—understanding thereby the native depravity or enmity of the human heart against God—and thus leaves on the minds of men a deep sense of their absolute helplessness because of sin. The New School man, *conceding* man's moral inability—understanding thereby a fixed unwillingness to render obedience to God's law—affirms most earnestly his complete natural ability, understanding thereby that he comes into this world fully equipped with all that is necessary to qualify him for keeping perfectly God's commandments, and hence teaches the proposition "that there is nothing to hinder a man's loving God, and obeying him perfectly, but his own unwillingness,"—"that ability is commensurate with responsibility." From such instructions the sinner goes away with the belief that he can be perfectly holy the moment he chooses. At present those who are really solicitous to teach men their dependence on God for converting and sanctifying grace, discard this ancient distinction as embarrassing and likely to convey erroneous views in spite of all the care the preacher can take. Of this class Dr. Woods is a notable example. In plain Scripture language, he teaches man's inability in the broadest and most absolute sense, and points out his desperate wickedness or depravity of nature as that in which it consists. There are those among the "orthodox," whose views on this subject and modes of presenting it agree with those of Dr. Woods.

There is, however, reason to believe that the prevailing theology on this subject is something very different. We may ascertain it with a good degree of accuracy, by examining the teachings of the theological seminaries.

Dr. Tyler, of East Windsor, Conn.—president of a seminary founded for the express purpose of maintaining a testimony for truth betrayed at New Haven—in a recent sermon, preached and published with the view of correcting what he deemed erroneous opinions gaining currency in that neighborhood, affirms as his main proposition, that "God does not require of man what he has no power to do." In his discussion he concedes man's inability, but places it altogether in want of inclination to obedience. Throughout his entire discourse he gives great prominence to man's natural ability, and adduces a variety of considerations to prove it. The whole drift of his argument is to lessen, or explain away man's inability, and exalt his ability. The tendency of the discourse is to weaken in the mind of the sinner the sense of dependence on divine grace. Dr. Harvey—an Old School Presbyterian of Thompsonville—took the professor to task for his sermon.

Dr. Tyler replied, assuring Dr. Harvey that all he meant in vindicating man's natural ability, was to teach that he is a free agent. Whereupon Dr. Harvey reads him a timely lecture on the proper use of terms, and suggests the propriety of employing language that will convey his meaning, and not something the very opposite. Dr. Tyler published another sermon a good many years ago, in which he lays down as his main proposition, that "there is nothing to hinder the salvation of any man but his own will." In the same discourse he affirms "that man has perfect ability to comply with the terms of salvation, if he will." In another sermon, published about the same time, he uses the following language: "How many hear the gospel, upon whom it produces no salutary effect. And why? Not because they are incapable of yielding to the motives of the gospel, but because they resist those motives." "It will not avail the sinner to plead he has no power to obey. He has power. If he has power to sin, he has power to cease from sinning—if he has power to rebel against God, he has power to submit to God. He has all the power he needs: all indeed, which he can possess. If God were to renew his heart this moment, his power would not be increased; he would only be willing to use aright the power which he now abuses and perverts." "When God works in men to will and to do, it is not to enable men to do their duty; but to incline them to do what they are able to do and what they ought to do without any supernatural divine influence." In time the Doctor was quoted by the Congregationalist as favoring the New School theology.* Soon after he comes forward with sundry explanations, seemingly intended to show that his true meaning was something very different from what his language imports. In the recent controversy, growing out of the Enfield case, he avowed views on this subject which Old School men generally will accept as sound. Yet if we are to take his published sermons as specimens of his method of teaching the doctrine, there can be but little doubt but that his influence contributes to swell the tide of error on this subject.

The position occupied by Prof. Park renders it particularly important to ascertain his views and teachings on this subject. Dr. Dana says:—"His views of human ability are extravagant and extreme. They obviously tend to foster in man a spirit of pride, of self-sufficiency, of independence on God, and emphatically of procrastination."† In his Convention sermon and appended notes, he plainly teaches man's ability to be commensurate with his responsibility, and places this inability, of which he is subject, in his unwillingness. In his controversy with Prof. Hodge, he entered into a long and labored argument to prove that the Edwardean divines, in affirming man's natural ability, "meant *something more* than that he is

* Cong. Nov. 21, 1851. † Remonstrance, p. 24.

possessed of natural capacities of soul and body." He quotes, with approbation, the following from Dr. Emmons:—"Unrenewed men are as able to do right, as to do wrong; and to do their duty, as to neglect their duty; to love God as to hate God, to choose life as to choose death; to walk in the narrow way to life, as in the broad way to hell;" "as able to embrace the gospel as a thirsty man is to drink water, or a hungry man to eat the most delicious food." "They can love God, repent of sin, and believe in Christ, and perform every religious duty, as well as they can think, or speak, or walk." And the following from Dr. Smalley:—"It must be granted that we do generally suppose a man's present duty cannot exceed his present *strength*, suppose it to have been impaired by what means it may." "*And this*," says Prof. Park, "*is the common representation of the 'Exercise School.'*" "It is the common remark of the Edwardean school, that men have no inability to repent except their unwillingness." "The doctrine of New England is, that any powerlessness in the original, literal, proper meaning of the word, is incompatible with obligation."* Such is the theology taught in the most prominent theological seminary, and in the leading theological quarterly in New England.

On this subject the influence of East Windsor and Andover seem to be in the same direction.

* Bib. Sac., Jan., 1852.

The New Haven theology is well known. Most likely no antagonism exists at Bangor. Prof. Pond would hardly find any good reason for rejecting the language of his ancient instructor, Dr. Emmons.

The Boston Congregationalist, under date of Decemeer 14, 1849, has the following language in its editorial columns in relation to the answer in the Catechism to the question—"Is any man able perfectly to keep the commandments of God?"—"It *cannot* be true that we are *not able* to keep that law. We need no better proof that we *can* keep it than the simple fact that God requires us to do so. We have always regarded the above answer in the Catechism as conveying an idea which either is not intended, or if intended, is altogether false and unsound in theology. That no mere man *can possibly* keep the divine law in this life, is by no means true." This language is clear and explicit.

The Doctrinal Book and Tract Society teach, in No. 23 of their series, that the Holy Spirit is necessary merely because men are unwilling to receive the gospel. "Had they a willing mind, the work would be done."* In No. 8 we find the following language:—"A sinful man *can* become holy—the non-elect *can* comply with the terms of the gospel—they are just as able to repent and believe the gospel as the elect—as capable of do-

*p. 7.

ing right as doing wrong—it is proper to say they can do what they are willing to do."*

These views, there can be no doubt, prevail among the orthodox in New England.

VI. *Christ's Satisfaction.*

The doctrine of the Westminster Standards on this subject is expressed in the following terms:—"The Lord Jesus, by his perfect obedience and sacrifice of himself, which he through the Eternal Spirit once offered up to God, has fully satisfied the justice of his father: and purchased not only reconciliation, but an everlasting inheritance in the kingdom of heaven for all those whom the father hath given unto him."† This is usually regarded as the doctrine, substantially set forth by Dr. Woods in his published lectures. It will also be difficult to make good a charge of heresy on this subject against Dr. Hopkins. His neighbor, Dr. Stiles, a thorough going old-Calvinist, while finding fault with some of Hopkins' disciples, for "denying a real vicarious suffering in Christ's atonement," admitted that Hopkins himself "differed from them, and held the atonement in a just and scriptural sense." Edwards and all the great orthodox divines who preceded him in New England, taught the doctrine of the Confession. Even yet there are those who believe it and preach it.

*p. 4. †Chap. viii: Sect. 5.

Dr. Woods, however, informs us that erroneous opinions on this subject exist among the orthodox. He states them in the following terms:—"Christ did not die in the place of sinners, as a vicarious sacrifice, to satisfy divine justice and procure the forgiveness of sins, but merely to make an affecting demonstration of God's perfect readiness to save sinners, and by a striking instance of patience and quiet submission in suffering to win their hearts to love and obedience."* From other sources we learn that the New England doctrine of the atonement is something different from that which formerly prevailed, very nearly identical with what Dr. Woods calls an erroneous opinion. Dr. Pond throws much valuable light on the subject. He says:—"The doctrine of atonement, which seems not to have been touched by President Edwards, except as involved in the more general subject of redemption, was very lucidly treated by his son, and by Rev. Dr. West, of Stockbridge. To these men, more than to any others, are the theologians of New England indebted for the clear and consistent views which now generally prevail in relation to this vital topic. The distinction between atonement and redemption; the universality of the former as to its sufficiency, and the particularity of the latter as to its application; the entire consistency between full satisfaction, on the one hand, and free grace in

* Puritan Theology, p. 41.

forgiveness on the other; these are points, which, so far as I know, had never been clearly stated and established, previous to the publications of the younger Edwards and of Dr. West."*

Dr. Pond gives us to understand that the views which now generally prevail, on this subject, are more clear and consistent than the ancient doctrine and authorizes us to look to Dr. Edwards as their expounder. It is therefore important to ascertain what are the teachings of that celebrated divine. They are fully set forth in his Sermons on the Atonement—"preached before His Excellency the Governor, and a large number of both houses of the legislature of the State of Connecticut, during their sessions at New Haven, in October, 1785, and published by request." The difficulty of reconciling the great truth that forgiveness of sins is in consequence of the riches of Divine grace, with the commonly received doctrine of the atonement, led him to endeavor after some other view of the subject, that would not be exposed to these difficulties. "If the sinner's debt be paid, how does it appear that there is any pardon or grace in his deliverance?" he asks. "By this difficulty," he says in his introduction to the discussion of this subject, "some have been induced to reject the doctrine of Christ's redemption, satisfaction, or atonement. Others who have not been driven to that extremity by this difficulty, yet have been ex-

* Sketches, etc., No. 5.

ceedingly perplexed and embarrassed. Of these last I freely admit myself to have been one. Having from my youth devoted myself to the study of theoretic and practical theology, I have regarded this as one of the GORDIAN KNOTS in that science." His theory he regards as a solution of the problem. The Gordian knot he professes to untie, not cut. While he maintains that we are forgiven through the atonement of Christ, and can be forgiven in no other way, he also asserts as a principle fundamental to his theory, that "the atonement does not consist in the payment of a debt, properly so called." The reason why an atonement is necessary to the pardon of a sinner is the same why his punishment would have been necessary if no atonement had been made. It is necessary, as he says, to maintain the dignity and authority of the lawgiver, as well as the consistency between the legislative and executive departments of his government. His definition of the atonement corresponds with his reasons for its necessity. "It consists," he says, "in doing that which, for the purpose of establishing the authority of the Divine law, and of supporting in due time the Divine government, is equivalent to the punishment of the sinner according to the letter of the law." Although he speaks of Christ as a substitute for sinners, yet he does not use the term in the sense in which it is ordinarily employed by Calvinistic writers discussing this subject. His meaning is that the atonement is the substitute for the punishment threatened in the law, and was intended to accomplish the same ends in relation to God's law and government. He does not teach that Christ, standing in the "room and stead" of his elect, pays their debt, or endures the penalty due to their sins; his sufferings and death, however, he regards as equivalent to the eternal punishment of the sinner, as far as the maintenance of the authority and dignity of his law and government is concerned.

In expounding the doctrine of the atonement, he speaks of three kinds of justice—*commutative*, *distributive*, and *general*. Commutative justice, he says, respects property, and requires that every man should receive the payment of his debts. Now the atonement, he pleads, has no respect to this kind of justice at all. It is not the payment of any of our debts. It does not, therefore, satisfy commutative justice. Distributive justice has respect to man's personal character or conduct, and requires that virtue, or good conduct, should be rewarded, and crimes, or vicious conduct, punished. The atonement, he claims, has no respect whatever to this kind of justice, since man just as much deserves punishment as though Christ had made no atonement. If Christ, by his sufferings and death, had satisfied distributive justice, then, he argues, forgiveness would not have been of grace, but of debt—nothing more than man's due. But the atonement does not satisfy this kind of justice; and hence, he reasons, forgiveness is a grace, a free gift, because, notwithstanding the atonement, man deserves death just as much as if Christ had never died. General or public justice, he says, comprehends all moral goodness, and requires that the thing which is right be done. To practise justice, in this sense of the term, is to act agreeably to the dictates of general benevolence. And the pardon of the sinner is, according to this view of the subject, an act of justice, because it is undoubtedly most conducive to the divine glory and general good of the created system, that every believer in Christ should be pardoned. The atonement satisfies this kind of justice, because it was right and proper that it should be made, and tends to the greatest good of intelligent beings. This sense of the word justice is, however, he tells us, an improper one, and hence he claims that the atonement, in no proper sense of the term, satisfies justice, nor is forgiveness an act of justice. Dr. Edwards regarded the efficiency of the atonement as consisting in this, that, in consequence of it, God can pardon and save sinners, and still maintain the dignity and authority of his government. It secures nothing. It only opens up the way for God's mercy and grace to go forth. *How* it operates to accomplish this end, he does not tell us. His theory renders necessary a departure from the common phraseology on the subject; yet he still uses it to a considerable extent, and thus not unfrequently seems to teach a doctrine different from that which he really holds.

Such are what Prof. Pond styles "the clear and consistent views now generally prevalent on this vital topic."

Dr. Emmons' views very nearly accord with those of Dr. Edwards. A few propositions will clearly set them forth. All that was necessary was that the way should be opened up, whereby God, consistently with his justice, could forgive sin. If a substitute would suffer in the room of sinners God's justice would be appeased, and the obstacles in the way of his exercising pardoning grace removed. Christ became this substitute, endured the needful suffering, and thus atoned for sin. Christ's obedience to the law was no part of his mediatorial work—further than it qualified him for suffering, as the lamb must needs be without blemish. The entire efficacy of his sufferings was to open the way for the forgiveness of sins. God, in consequence, can offer salvation to all mankind, and bestow it upon all penitent, believing, returning sinners. All that the believer receives for Christ's sake is forgiveness. Christ did not endure the penalty due to sinners—he did not endure any punishment at all—he did not pay the debt sinners owed to God, either of suffering or obedience. The doctrine of a limited atonement he rejected totally, contending Christ's death had the same favorable aspect on the non-elect as the elect. He denied that Christ *merited* any thing for sinners. The very phrase, merits of Christ, he discarded as unscriptural and improper. He says:

"It is often designedly or undesignedly used to convey the idea that Christ, by his obedience and sufferings on the cross, paid the debt of suffering and obedience in the room of sinners, so that God is obliged, in point of justice, to release them from eternal sufferings, and bestow upon them eternal life. This is a false and unscriptural sentiment, and naturally tends to lead men into several other great and dangerous errors."* "Though Christ suffered the just for the unjust, though he made his soul an offering for sin, and though he suffered most excruciating pains in the garden and on the cross, yet he did not lay God under the least obligation to pardon and save a single sinner."†

The views of Emmons, on some subjects, are not received by many in New England. His doctrine of the atonement, however, does not appear here to meet with any opposition. Dr. Dwight's views of the atonement conform substantially to those of the younger Edwards, nor do they differ materially from those of Emmons. His definition clearly exhibits the sense in which he held the doctrine. "The atonement consists in making sufficient amends for the faults which men have committed, and placing the law and government of God in such a situation that when sinners are pardoned, both shall be equally honorable and efficacious as before."‡ Christ was a substitute, equally of all mankind. He no more atoned for

* Works, Vol. V., p. 35. † Id. p. 25. ‡ Dwight's Theology, Vol. II., p. 206.

the elect than for the damned. He did not pay the debt his people owed to God; he only made such amends for the sins and faults of men, that God might honorably pardon and save whom he would. The atonement secured nothing; it only rendered salvation possible. The obedience of Christ was essentially concerned in the atonement, but only as qualifying him to work it out. It was necessary that Christ should be holy, that he might be a fit Mediator. Such is the atonement Dwight teaches. He does not give the obedience of Christ the prominence, or hold it in the sense customary among Calvinistic divines. He does not exhibit it as needful to merit eternal life for those for whom Christ atoned by his sufferings, nor does he assign it any separate, independent fuuction; he subordinates it altogether to his propitiatory sufferings. He expressly says:—"The attempts made to discriminate between these parts of Christs's mediation, and to assign to each its exact proportion of influence in the economy of redemption, seem to me to have been very partially successful."* Dr. Dwight has exerted a powerful influence over the New England mind.

In 1823, James Murdock, D. D., Professor in the Theological Seminary at Andover, published a sermon on the "Nature of the Atonement." "The sermon was delivered," he tells us, in his advertisement, "to an audience composed chiefly of

* Dwight's Theology, Vol. II., p. 216.

theological students, and designed to aid them in forming their opinions on the important subject discussed." This fact, together with the position of the author, renders the sermon peculiarly important as a source of information on the subject in hand. The following brief extracts, it is believed, fairly exhibit his doctrine. "The atonement must be something different from the execution of the law itself: because it is to be a substitute for it, something which will render it safe and proper to suspend the regular course of distributive justice." "The atonement was in the nature of it an exhibition of the righteousness of God. It did not consist in an execution of the law on any being whatever, for it was a substitute for an execution of it." "It did not fulfil the law or satisfy its demands on transgressors." "Its immediate influence was not on the characters and relations of men, as transgressors, nor on the claims of the law upon them. Its direct operation was on the feelings and the apprehensions of the beings at large who are under the moral government of God." "The atonement was a public exhibition; and such an exhibition as would impress all the creatures of God with a deep and awful sense of the majesty and sanctity of his law, of the criminality of disobedience to it, and of the holy, unbending rectitude of God as a moral governor." "It represented these things *symbolically*." "It did not satisfy the demands of the violated law upon the sinner." "All that it could do was to display the feelings of God in regard to his law: and secure by the impression it made the public objects, which would be gained by an execution of the law. It did not cancel any of the claims of the law upon us. And hence after the atonement was made God was under no legal obligations to exempt any man from punishment. If he had never pardoned a single transgressor, neither law nor distributive justice would have been contravened. And if he pardons at all, it is mere grace. Or to state it otherwise, the atonement was not of such a nature as to require God to pardon us, but it enables him to do it, with credit to himself and safety to his kingdom." Such were the views taught at Andover twenty-two years ago. They were opposed, however. Prof. Stuart, it is said, published two discourses to counteract their influence; and Dr. Woods, filling, as he did, the chair of Professor of Christian theology, could hardly have been silent. There must have been collisions, even in the pulpit of the Seminary. It might be difficult, however, to point out any real difference between the doctrine of Murdock on the one hand, and of Edwards the younger, Emmons and Dwight, on the other.

Prof. Park, in a note to his convention sermon, declares his dissent from the views of Symington, and gives the following as his own definition of the atonement:—" A true representation seems to be, that although Christ has not literally paid the debt of sinners, nor literally borne their punishment, nor satisfied the legislative nor the remunerative justice of God in any such sense or degree as itself to make it *obligatory* on him to save any sinners, yet the atonement has such a relation to the whole moral government of God as to make it *consistent* with the honor of his legislative and retributive justice to save all men, and to make it essential to the highest honor of his benevolence or general justice to renew and save some. Therefore it satisfies the law and justice of God in such a sense as to render it proper for him to offer salvation to all men, bestow it upon all who will accept it, and cause those to accept it for whom the interests of the universe will allow him to interpose his regenerating grace." Dr. Dana represents Prof. Park as "maintaining that it cannot be said Christ's passive obedience frees us from punishment, and that in case of the penitent the demands of the law are evaded or waved."* Prof. Park would hardly take exception to the doctrine of Dr. Murdock's sermon.

Tract No. 8 of the series issued by the Doctrinal Book and Tract Society, uses the following language:—"God has provided a full and complete atonement for all the sins of all mankind." "The atonement of Christ is sufficient for all, offered to all, and irrespective of the divine purpose as to its effectual application made as much for one

* Remonstrance, p. 9

man as another." "It has never yet been proved that Christ died exclusively for the elect." These testimonies justify us in concluding that while some may hold to an atonement such as is taught in the Confession and Catechisms, the prevailing theology teaches rather a symbolical transaction, efficacious in securing the salvation of none, but only in opening up the way for the consistent exercise of mercy on God's part, and which has of course the same favorable aspect on the non-elect as the elect.

VIII. *Regeneration, Conversion, Effectual Calling.*

That change by which the sinner is united to Christ is in the Confession and Catechisms termed "effectual calling." This phrase has gone very much out of use in New England. "Regeneration" and "conversion" are more commonly employed. Dr. Pond says:—"Our ministers do not merge regeneration in effectual calling." The Confession of Faith states the doctrine on this subject in the following terms:—"All the elect, God is pleased, effectually to call, by his word and Spirit out of that state of sin and death in which they are by nature to grace and salvation by Jesus Christ; enlightening their minds spiritually and savingly to understand the things of God; taking away their heart of stone and giving them a heart of flesh; renewing their wills and by his almighty power determining them to that which is good and effectually drawing them to Jesus Christ, yet so as they come most freely, being made willing by his grace." "Man is altogether passive therein, until, being quickened and renewed by the Holy Spirit, he is thereby enabled to answer this call and to embrace the grace offered and conveyed in it."* Such was the ancient doctrine of New England. Dwight and Woods, together with those who hold the old doctrine of a depraved nature antecedent to sinful actions, still maintain, substantially, the same principles. Those, however, who with the New Haven and Andover men deny antecedent depravity hold peculiar views as to regeneration. The New Haven divines maintain that the term regeneration is to be understood in two senses—the theological and popular. In the first sense it denotes a change in the governing purpose of the mind; and is that act of the mind, by which the sinner, prompted by self-love, chooses God as his portion or chief good. In the last or popular sense, it denotes a process, or series of acts and states of mind, and includes all those acts which they denominate "Using the means of regeneration." They maintain that antecedent to regeneration, in the restricted or theological sense, the selfish principle is suspended in the sinner's heart, that the sinner then ceases to sin, and is in a state of neutrality,

*Chap. X: Sect. 1 and 2.

and that in this state he uses the means of regeneration with motives which are neither right nor wrong—he takes into solemn consideration the question whether the highest happiness is to be found in God or in the world—he pursues this inquiry until it results in the conviction that such happiness is to be found in God only. He follows up the conviction with engrossing contemplation, till he discovers an excellence in divine objects which excites him to make desperate efforts to give his heart to God; and in this process of thought, of effort, and of action, he perseveres till it results in a change of heart. Thus they, in fact, represent regeneration as a gradual and progressive work. They also maintain that the sinner may so resist the grace of God as to render it impossible for God to convert him. That this representation is correct, will be abundantly evident to any one who will carefully examine the Christian Spectator for 1829, pp. 16, 17, 18, 19, 32, 33, 227. They deny, in the most explicit terms, that there is any change in the nature or disposition of the sinner antecedent to the exercise of right affections. "As to those who hold to the infusion of something into the soul previous, either in the order of time or nature to the first right affection, and as a sort of fountain from which such affection is to flow, we should only say, that although we do not impute to them the blasphemy, yet we cannot wholly acquit them of the absurdity of Gibbon, who, in pretending to describe the manner in which the primitive teachers were inspired, says they were mere organs of the Spirit, just as the pipe or flute is of him who blows it."* They admit the agency of the Spirit in regeneration, yet they maintain that its influence is altogether persuasive, exerted through the medium of truth or motives. "Indeed we know," say they, "of no other effectual hold which this divine agent can have on the sinner, whom he would turn from the error of his ways, but that which consists in *so* bringing the truths of the Bible into contact with his understanding and sensibilities that he shall voluntarily shun the threatened evil, and choose the proffered good."† "This influence he can resist, and thus harden his heart against God."‡ "Free moral agents can do wrong under all possible preventing influence."§ "I do not believe," says Dr. Taylor, in his letter to Dr. Hawes, "that the grace of God can be truly said to be irresistible in the primary, proper import of the term: but I do believe that in all cases it may be resisted by man as a free agent; and that when it does become effectual to conversion, it is *unresisted.*" Such, substantially, are the views of Finney, (who is understood to speak the sentiments of the New Haven divines,) as set forth in his sermon entitled "Sinners bound to change their own hearts." As far therefore as the theology of New Haven extends this is the doctrine which prevails.

* Christ. Spect. 1833, p. 361. † Ib. p. 356. ‡ Ib. 1831, p. 637. § Ib. 1830, p. 563.

Dr. Dana intimates that Prof. Park regards it as a change in the balance of the susceptibilities.* The Professor himself declares that in regeneration a nature inclining to sin, but not sinful, is changed into a nature inclining to holiness, but not holy, and that by the omnipotence of the regenerating Spirit.† The editors of the Congregationalist, after quoting from Calvinistic divines, with the view of exhibiting the Old School doctrine on this subject, reason thus:—"The statements which precede will enable any one to judge how great is the change which has taken place among many New England divines on this point. It amounts to an entire revolution. The theory of passivity in regeneration has been rejected, and the Synergistic theory adopted in its place. Of this we have a striking illustration in the tracts written by various New England divines for the Doctrinal Tract Society. On p. 3, of No. 27, it is taught that the Scriptures represent men 'as acting and being acted upon in their regeneration or conversion.' On p. 7 there is an argument against such as hold that man is 'merely *passive* in regeneration.' On p. 15 it is said, 'The sinner is not passive, but active in regeneration.' In Tract No. 3, the ascription to the orthodox of the doctrine that regeneration is 'the sole act of God' is treated as a slander, and the doctrine is taught that God renovates us 'by the use of means and motives

*Remonstrance, p. 8. †Bib. Sacra, XXXI. p. 627.

which leave us as free in conversion and new obedience as we ever were in transgression.' "* In a subsequent number they affirm that Dr. Woods and Dr. Tyler coincided in teaching that man is active and coöperates with God in regeneration, and thus are at variance with the Westminster divines; but nevertheless stand on the platform of sound and orthodox New England divines. They also labor to show that Jonathan Edwards taught the same doctrine.†

Rev. Mr. Eells, of Newburyport, thus forcibly describes the prevalent theology on this subject:—"It is action only that needs renovation. 'Regeneration is a change from sinful action to holy action.' 'All the work of the Spirit of God is reduced to mere persuasion. He may bring the truth home with power on the understanding and conscience, but he cannot change the heart. And, indeed, there is no heart to be changed. After all the work of the Spirit it remains in the power of man to yield or refuse, as he pleases, so that the glory of the change is all his own. It is not God that makes men to differ. It is their own work.' These are the doctrines taught by professors of theology—that are preached from the pulpit in this land of the Pilgrims. The evil is wide-spread, and is fast extending itself. *This is an undeniable truth.*"‡

* April 12, 1850. † Dec. 19, 1851. ‡ Sermons, p. 36, 37.

These testimonies will enable the reader to understand the views of regeneration and conversion that prevail in New England.

IX. *Justification.*

The Confession of Faith teaches that: "Those whom God effectually calleth he also freely justifieth; not by infusing righteousness into them, but by pardoning their sins and by accounting and accepting their persons as righteous; not for any thing wrought in them or done by them, but for Christ's sake alone; not by imputing faith itself, the act of believing, or any other evangelical obedience to them as their righteousness; but by imputing the obedience and satisfaction of Christ unto them, they receiving and resting on him and his righteousness by faith; which faith they have not of themselves: it is the gift of God."* The Catechism defines justification as "an act of God's free grace, whereby he pardoneth all our sins, and accepts us as righteous in his sight only for the righteousness of Christ imputed to us and received by faith alone."† There is no difficulty in understanding the doctrine of these propositions. It is clear and well defined. This too was the primitive doctrine among the churches of New England. The Synods of 1648 and 1680 affirmed

* Confession, Chap. XI. Sec. 1. † Ques. 33.

it. Norton, and Willard, and Edwards, and Bellamy all taught it. Nor can a charge of heresy on this point be made good against Hopkins. But what is the present faith of New England? We must learn it from the teachings of her leading Doctors.

Dr. Woods, after examining minutely the Scriptures which speak of justification, concludes thus: "And we are sure the apostle meant to teach us this momentous doctrine, namely, that sinners cannot be justified by works of obedience to the law; that if we are justified, it must be by grace, on the ground of the righteousness of Christ received by faith; and that good works, however important or indispensable on other accounts, are excluded from any influence as the meritorious ground of our justification before God."* He speaks of God treating men in justification as though they had never sinned, as though they were not ungodly. The mediatorial work of Christ—his obedience and death—he represents as the ground or meritorious condition of our forgiveness and acceptance with God. Our perfect obedience would, according to the law, have been the ground of our acceptance with God and enjoyment of the blessings of his kingdom. This ground of acceptance is wanting. But the obedience and death of our Redeemer come in place of it, and on this ground we enjoy the same favor

*Works, Vol. III. p. 165.

with God and the same blessedness as we should have done on the ground of our own obedience.* Christ's work as Redeemer does, alone, form *the perfect, meritorious condition, or ground of our justification before God,* nothing else being needed or admitted as a condition or any part of a condition *in that respect.*† He makes some interesting remarks in relation to justification through the imputed righteousness of Christ. He affirms it to be the doctrine of orthodox Protestants generally. "Yet," he says, "this doctrine, or rather this manner of stating it, has for some time past been objected to by ministers of the gospel in this country, chiefly in New England. And many ministers and laymen, who have not come to a decision on the subject, have an apprehension that this form of the doctrine must be given up." The reason of this dissent he finds to be that the doctrine is thought to imply that there is a literal transfer of moral character or personal attributes from one to another. The doctrine, however, he affirms, never had any such meaning as this. There is no reason, either from the Scriptures or from standard Calvinistic divines, to understand the word *impute* in this manner. When the righteousness of Christ is said to be imputed to us, the meaning is not that it properly belongs to us as our own personal righteousness, but that it is so reckoned to us, or put to our account, that we

* Works, Vol. III. p. 177. † Ib. p. 180.

share the benefits of it, or are treated as though we were righteous. He pleads that the meaning put upon the doctrine by some late New England divines, is unauthorized. He says that the most learned and discriminating of orthodox divines, both Lutheran and Calvinistic, take special pains to show that the imputation of Christ's righteousness to us does not imply that his righteousness is transferred to us, or infused into us, so as to become our personal attribute, but only that we partake of its benefit—that his righteousness is ours *imputatively.* He advocates the use of the "imputation" phraseology, and exhorts his brethren to hold fast the form of sound words.* This is the theology taught in Dr. Woods' published lectures.

Prof. Stuart, his distinguished colleague throughout his entire professorial career, did not accord with him entirely on this subject. His views are set forth in his Commentary on the Epistles to the Romans. The following extracts exhibit them fully. Remarking on the 5th chapter and 19th verse he says:—"Though I can scarcely entertain a doubt, that the *obedience* of Christ in this connection of thought means in particular his obedience in assuming our nature and his suffering an expiatory death in it, yet I would not exclude the idea that the *active* (as well as passive) obedience of his whole life contribute, yea was necessary to the perfection of his character as a Media-

* Works, Vol. III. pp. 201, 207.

tor, and a great High Priest who should make atonement for us. Without such obedience, he would have needed an atonement for himself instead of being able to make it for others. But in respect to the pacific allegation, 'that Christ's obedience is *imputed* to us': this Paul does not here, nor elsewhere, say, nor any other sacred writer. This is a phraseology superinduced upon the Bible, many years since the Reformation, from human systems and methods of explanation; and not one which is taken from the Scriptures and transferred into symbols. *In all the Bible there occurs* NOT *such a declaration, as that one man's sin or righteousness is* IMPUTED *to another.* (The italics are the Professors). The *thing* for substance aimed at by many, who employ such phraseology is doubtless a doctrine of the Bible, viz. that the obedience of Christ, above all his obedience unto death, did contribute to constitute him an all-glorious and all-sufficient Mediator. As to the rest, *that God* FOR CHRIST'S SAKE forgives sinners, not imputing their trespasses unto them, is the very sum and substance of what is appropriately called THE GOSPEL, and all which can exegetically be made out from the simple interpretation of the Scriptures. For in what part of the Bible is it said that *Christ obeyed for us?* Or where, that *his obedience is imputed to us?* And yet that *on our account* or *in our behalf*, he obeyed and suffered, I believe to be a great and fundamental doctrine of the Gospel."

In his excursus on the same passage he says: "Believers are made really and veritably holy in part (not putatively so) by the sanctifying influences of the Spirit of God, on account of what Christ has done and suffered; so that their holiness is not in this case factitious, and the Redeemer's holiness is not veritably theirs. If it were so, then *perfect* holiness would be theirs; and they could then present a claim of salvation on the ground of meeting the demands of the law. Mere *imputed* holiness, however, can never answer proper legal demands, and therefore it can never entitle the sinner to a proper legal acquittal. Pardon is given, altogether of *grace;* not on the ground of either real or factitious, i. e. imputed obedience. The first of these sinners cannot plead; the second the law does not in itself admit. If any one should reply, as doubtless some may do, that Christ is and is called *the Lord our Righteousness,* my reply is that he is at the same time called *our wisdom, and sanctification and redemption.* Now he is by this representation made just as much our imputed wisdom, and our imputed sanctification, and our imputed redemption as he is our imputed righteousness."* Prof. Stuart objects very emphatically to the language of the Westminster standards on the subject. He can hardly, however, be regarded as still holding the same doctrine. He uniformly speaks of justification as

* Commentary, p. 583.

gratuitous. An expression above quoted well sets forth his uniform teachings: "Pardon is given altogether of *grace not on the* GROUND *of either real or* IMPUTED OBEDIENCE." When therefore he teaches us that God *forgives sinners for Christ's sake*, we are not to understand him as meaning that what Christ has done and suffered is the ground on which he proceeds. The Professor's doctrine is about this: Christ by his atonement, for making which his holy life was a necessary qualification, removed the difficulties in the way of God's saving sinners, and now God, in the exercise of his sovereign mercy, bestows pardon and acceptance on the believer, without any particular respect to a law satisfying righteousness as the ground of his procedure. His influence is doubtless in opposition to the ancient doctrine of New England, set forth in the Westminster symbols.

Professor Murdock, in his Sermon on the Atonement, set forth his views of justification:—"Justification is not founded on the principles of law and distributive justice. It is an *absolute pardon*, an act of *mere grace;* and of grace on the part of God the Father, as well as on that of God the Son. For the operation of Christ's sacrifice, it appears, was not on the regular course of distributive justice in regard to individual transgressors. Its influence was on the public feeling respecting the character of God. And it only enabled God, with honor to himself, and safety to his kingdom, to gratify the desires of his heart by the pardon of repenting sinners. Justification is therefore a real departure from the regular course of justice; and such a departure from it as leaves the claims of the law on the persons justified, forever unsatisfied."* The views of Murdock and Stuart were about the same. Their methods of statement may differ; but not their doctrine. Diverse theologies, on this subject, must have been taught at Andover from the foundation of the Seminary.

Nor does Dr. Dwight's exhibition of this doctrine come up to the ancient standards. To say the least of it, it is exceedingly defective. Gospel justification is not forensic in its nature; it only closely resembles it; so thinks Dr. Dwight. "It consists," says he, "in the three following things: Pardoning the believer's sins, acquitting him from the punishment which they have deserved, and entitling him to the rewards or blessings due by law to perfect obedience only."† All these are given to the sinner out of the free and sovereign love of the Father, Son, and Holy Ghost—given without respect to any ground or consideration on which the act proceeds, but simply of divine grace. The work of Christ was efficient in removing the obstacles in the way of such procedure, and in doing no more. According to his views of the subject, he cannot admit the doctrine of the imputation of Christ's righteousness; and hence very properly banishes it from his system. Dwight's justifica-

*p. 30. †Dwight's Theology, Vol. II. p. 301.

tion is without any righteousness whatever. It must be admitted, however, that he carefully guards against the idea of justification being grounded on human merit. He clearly and fully teaches it to be of grace. Nor does he make faith itself the righteousness. He represents it as being only that on the exercise of which these blessings are given.*

Dr. Emmons also taught a doctrine on this subject, far different from that of the Catechism. *Justification*, in his judgment, "signifies no more nor less than the pardon or remission of sin."† He represents it at one time as an act, taking place the moment the sinner believes. Again, he speaks of it as conditional on perseverance in faith and obedience, (which condition is by divine grace always fulfilled in the case of every genuine believer,) and uses language which would seem to teach the doctrine that justification is not complete until death, or until the required conditions are actually fulfilled.‡ He further teaches that forgiveness comes through the mediation of Christ, and is on the ground of his atonement—that God bestows no other favor on man on this ground—that other blessings are bestowed in consequence of the atonement, not on the ground of it—a sinner being pardoned for Christ's sake is in a fit state for receiving other spiritual blessings on other grounds. He contended that there is no

* Dwight's Theology, Vol. II. p. 300,324. † Works, Vol. V. p. 44. ‡ Ib. p. 46.

propriety in directing sinners to go to Christ for regenerating or sanctifying grace, or for any thing but pardon, which is all that ministers have any authority to offer sinners through Christ.* The distinction of Christ's obedience into active and passive he pronounced unscriptural. The doctrine that believers are accepted as righteous, and entitled to eternal life, on the ground of Christ's imputed righteousness, he rejected as unreasonable and absurd. *Imputation* found no favor in his eyes. Eternal life, and all its implied blessings, are bestowed, according to his teachings, as the reward of the believer's own sincere obedience. God does not, he holds, bestow eternal life on believers because their sincere obedience atones for their sin, or because it merits eternal life, but because it is a proper ground, reason, or condition, for bestowing on them such a gracious and unmerited reward.† The doctrine that believers are rewarded, or receive eternal life, for Christ's obedience, as really and truly as they are forgiven for his atonement, he pronounces a *palpable absurdity*."‡ Such are the views of the "Sage of Franklin" in relation to the great matter of man's justification.

Prof. Park, according to Dr. Dana, teaches "that Christ needed obedience for himself, and could not perform a work of supererogation for others; that if Christ obeyed the law for us we need not obey

* Works, Vol. V. p. 46, 47. † Ib. p. 84, 86. ‡ Ib. p. 93.

it for ourselves, for that the law does not require two obediences; neither in this case is there any grace in our pardon; that Christ's obedience being imputed to us involves a double absurdity, etc."* We much regret that we have not access to any full statement of the Professor's views on this subject. Dr. Dana's testimony is, however, worthy of all confidence.

Mr. Eells says, in his Sermons, that the ancient doctrine of justification is almost wholly unknown among the descendants of the Puritans; and that men in high places in the church seem to find a malignant pleasure, first, in carricaturing it, and then in holding it up to derision and contempt.†

There are those who truly hold the doctrine of the Westminster standards on this subject, and state it in the language there employed; there are those, again, who accept the Westminster doctrine, but reject the Westminster phraseology, a class, smaller, it is thought, than many good men are willing to admit; the prevailing theology, however, it is believed, rejects both the ancient phraseology and the ancient doctrine; it teaches neither a justification by works, nor a justification on the ground of Christ's righteousness, but a justification, purely gratuitous, without direct respect to any righteousness whatever.

* Remonstrance, p. 9.

† Sermons, p. 33.

We have thus endeavored to give a candid exhibition of the Theology of New England in relation to Inspiration, Election, Man's connection with Adam, Sin and Depravity, Inability, Regeneration Conversion or Effectual Calling, the Atonement and Justification—the great doctrines of the Gospel. No more is needed, we conceive, to exhibit the peculiarities of the Theology of New England, although there are still other points, which it would be interesting to pass under review.

What, then, is the conclusion of the whole matter? It seems to be this:—There are some among the orthodox of New Englaud, who hold and teach the doctrines of the Westminster Confession of Faith, as held and taught by the puritan fathers. This class it is to be feared is not numerous.

There is another section of the orthodox, which must be regarded as holding and teaching, to all intents and purposes, the Arminianism of John Wesley. This class is increasing. The tendency of things seems to be to sink all doctrinal differences between Wesleyans and Calvinians.

That theology, however, which claims to be the theology of New England, embraces the great middle class. It teaches the decrees of God, a particular providence, election, and the perseverance of the saints, as taught by Calvinists generally. It rejects the imputation of Adam's sin and Christ's righteousness, and a limited, efficacious atonement. It asserts that man's ability is commensurate with his responsibility, and that his inability consists altogether in his unwillingness. On these points the great mass of New England divines seem to be agreed. As to the doctrine of sin, depravity, and regeneration, there exists a diversity of opinion. Some hold to a depravity of nature antecedent to actual sin, and to a regeneration by the Spirit, in which man is altogether passive. Others reject the doctrine of a sinful nature; assert that all sin consists in unholy or sinful exercises; and teach a regeneration, which is but a change in the governing purpose of the soul, or of the balance of the susceptibilities, or of a nature to sin, but not sinful, into a nature to holiness, but not holy. This is the theology of New Haven, Andover, and probably of Bangor also—the theology of the "Bibliotheca Sacra," the great New England quarterly—the theology of the Congregationalist—the theology, in short, of the influences that to a great extent control and determine public opinion all over the country—the theology, it is claimed, and would seem with good reason, of a very large majority of New England divines.

The prevailing theology in New England, at present, does not appear to be the theology of the Puritans.

It will hardly be denied by any, that the preceding statements are, in the main at least, correct. It may, however, be said, that these differences are of little, very little importance; the great essentials are held in common by both parties. While it is joyfully conceded, that much valuable truth is held even by those whose views are most erroneous, it cannot, we think, be admitted consistently with truth, that the differences specified are unimportant. The old and the new are not the same—either in their principles or their influence. If the one is truth, the other, in so far as it is another, is error. If the one is meat and drink to the soul, the other is spiritual poison. Whoever carefully examines these systems of doctrine, will see at once that in relation to some of the most momentous subjects that concern man's salvation, they are antagonistic. It cannot then be of little moment which is received into the heart, or which is proclaimed from our pulpits.

There is prevalent intense indifference to doctrinal truth. A popular liberality smiles complacently on every form of religious belief (except old fashioned orthodoxy,) and insists that one is just about as good as another. It is further to be feared, that there is very little, earnest, thorough, discriminating preaching of the truth, even as far as it is professedly received; that many subjects of vital importance to the soul, are seldom mentioned in the pulpit;—that many dangerous errors abound, against which, the warning voice of the watchmen on Zion's walls is seldom lifted. This state of things is far from consistent with that importance every where attached to doctrinal truth in God's word. Our Savior thought it necessary to caution his disciples in very pointed terms against the doctrine of the Pharisees and Sadducees. Paul reminded Timothy that, "All Scripture is given by inspiration of God, and is profitable for doctrine, for reproof, for correction, for instruction in righteousness, that the man of God may be perfect, thoroughly furnished unto all good works," at the same time exhorting him to "hold fast the form of sound words" he had received, and warning him against those who would not endure sound doctrine, but would, after their own lusts, heap to themselves teachers, having itching ears. The same apostle must have thought the truth as it is in Jesus of momentous importance when he thus wrote the Galatians: "But though we or an angel from heaven preach any other gospel unto you than that which we have preached unto you, let him be accursed. As we said before so say I now again, if any man preach any other gospel unto you than that ye have received let him be accursed." John, in his Epistle to the elect, lady expresses similar views:—"Whosoever transgresseth and abideth not in the doctrine of Christ hath not God. If there come any unto you and bring not this doctrine, receive him not into your house neither bid him God speed; for he that biddeth him God speed is partaker of his evil deeds." There is set forth in God's word a system, called at one time, the

"Gospel," at another the "Truth as it is in Jesus," at another the "Doctrine of Christ," and at still another the "Word of God." To this system of truth the Scriptures continually attach the very first importance. It is the sword of the Spirit—the wisdom of God and power of God unto salvation. It is this which the Spirit uses in converting the sinner, and in sanctifying and comforting the people of God. Nothing else is the sword of the Spirit; nothing else is the means of effecting the salvation of souls. God does not bless error. Nor does he honor a diluted, or a mutilated gospel. No other truth, however important, can accomplish the ends for which God has ordained the gospel of his grace. It alone will reform what is wrong among men, and save souls from eternal misery.

If these things be true, as they are beyond all controversy, then that indifference and that liberality already mentioned must be simply criminal in God's sight. If there is any thing in this world about which the church ought to be jealous, it is the purity, fulness and completeness of the doctrine proclaimed in our pulpits and issued from our press. If souls are converted and sanctified—edified to the highest degree—the truth as it is in Jesus, the whole truth and nothing but the truth, must be learned. Those who substitute something else for it, give famishing souls a stone instead of bread. Those who keep back a part are unfaithful to their Master, who has bidden them declare the whole counsel of God. Those who abandon important truth, leaving error to abound unopposed, must be regarded as traitors to their Lord. If ever the world is converted and the reign of righteousness inaugurated, it will not be by leaving out of sight the truth of the gospel—nor by abandoning whatever of it is offensive to the carnal mind—nor by the preaching of error;—not even by the proclamation of OTHER truth however important. It is only a pure gospel in its integrity—proclaimed with the simplicity with which it is set forth in the inspired volume, that will be the means of ushering in that glorious era. Most assuredly the church, styled the pillar and the ground of the truth is called upon to look well to the truth, it is her duty to maintain and propagate.

Let us then search the Scriptures. Let us go to the great Teacher and find out the truth. Let us hold it fast. Let us feed upon it ourselves. Let us send it—the bread and water of life—to the perishing world around us. Let us give our influence to the support and propagation of a pure gospel. Let no maxims of worldly prudence, no false liberality, induce us to aid in building up the cause of error. Let us consent to no theology so "comprehensive" as to embrace both truth and falsehood. Let us not be "children tossed to and fro and carried about with every wind of doctrine, by the sleight of men and cunning craftiness whereby they lie in wait to deceive; but speaking the truth in love, grow up into him in all things which is the head even Christ."

www.ingramcontent.com/pod-product-compliance
Lightning Source LLC
LaVergne TN
LVHW011120110826
845150LV00008B/2194